CLEVELAND ARENA

OHIO'S PROFESSIONAL BOXING MECCA 1937–1973

Pictured are miscellaneous fight tickets and press passes from Cleveland Arena's boxing days. (Author's collection.)

On the Front Cover: Down for the count! Hilton "Fitzie" Fitzpatrick lies battered on the canvas as Ezzard Charles strides away. Charles, who would go on to become world heavyweight champion, won by a fourth-round knockout (KO) at the December 2, 1947, Toyshop Fund Show. This was the second time Charles, nicknamed "The Cincinnati Cobra," had beaten Fitzpatrick in 1947. (Author's collection.)

On the Back Cover: This photograph shows a full house of fight fans at Cleveland Arena in 1943. (Courtesy of Michael Schwartz Library, Cleveland State University.)

CLEVELAND ARENA

OHIO'S PROFESSIONAL BOXING MECCA 1937–1973

Jerry Fitch

ARCADIA PUBLISHING

ISBN 978-1-4671-0806-5

Published by Arcadia Publishing
Charleston, South Carolina

Printed in the United States of America

Library of Congress Control Number: 2021949846

For all general information, please contact Arcadia Publishing:
Telephone 843-853-2070
Fax 843-853-0044
E-mail sales@arcadiapublishing.com
For customer service and orders:
Toll-Free 1-888-313-2665

Visit us on the Internet at www.arcadiapublishing.com

Contents

ACKNOWLEDGMENTS

As always, I must thank my friend Bill Chase, whose skills at research are always appreciated and needed.

I must also state that, unless otherwise noted, all of the photographs used in this book are from my personal collection, most of which I obtained from the *Plain Dealer* in the 1980s thanks to the then sports editor Thomas Greer. Award-winning sportswriter Bob Dolgan was instrumental in that process also. Most of those *Plain Dealer* photographs came from the Cleveland News Research Department. Autographed photographs and several others were given to me by the fighters shown in those images. Photographer credits are shown where available.

I was once again able to draw on the fantastic series written by Dan Taylor in 1952 for the *Cleveland Press*. His history of Cleveland boxing started on January 28 of that year and ran for 106 days. It proved to be a major source for my listings of fight action during the first 15 years of the arena. Dan Taylor was not only a writer, but he also did some local matchmaking.

I want to give special thanks to Jeff Ruetsche of Arcadia Publishing, who inspired me to write another book for the company. Ruetsche was my editor way back in 2001–2002 when I wrote *Cleveland's Greatest Fighters of All Time* for Arcadia.

My son Tad, whose own writing skills far surpass mine, is always an inspiration for me to keep on writing.

And last but certainly not least, my love, Lynda, is always in my corner and that means the world to me.

INTRODUCTION

Cleveland, like most cities, saw a ban on boxing in or around 1830. It was considered an illegal activity, and if one wanted to watch a boxing match, one had to find a secret venue, a barge, or maybe a private club. Fight fans were often seen running from the sheriff. The countrywide ban on boxing was not lifted locally until 1923. Even then only amateur boxing was allowed until finally in 1924 professional boxing was given the green light here.

In the early days fight cards were held in such places as the LaSalle Club, Charley Marotta's Gym at East Seventy-Ninth Street, and eventually in the city or Central Armory. By 1924, the Olympic Arena, an outdoor venue located at West Seventy-Third Street and Denison Avenue, held many boxing shows. Fights were also held at the Coliseum, which was located at East Forty-Sixth Street and Euclid Avenue. Cleveland Public Hall also became a regular site for boxing shows starting in the 1920s and continued on right into the Don King era.

Some other places where fights were held were Gray's Armory and the Taylor Bowl on Harvard Avenue and East Forty-Ninth Street. Walter Taylor, a local promoter, built this outdoor arena and held many very good shows there for several years.

There were also a few big shows held at League Park on Cleveland's east side. League Park was the home of Cleveland's professional baseball team, the Cleveland Indians, who won their first World Series there in 1920.

After Cleveland Municipal Stadium was built in 1931, various major fight cards were held there from time to time. The first event ever held at the new stadium was on July 3, 1931, when Max Schmeling stopped challenger Young Stribling with seconds remaining in the 15th round, retaining his world heavyweight championship.

In November 1937, the Cleveland Arena at East Thirty-Seventh Street and Euclid Avenue opened for business. It was the brainchild of local sports entrepreneur Al Sutphin, who built the arena for his hockey team, the Cleveland Barons. Previously, they had been playing at the much smaller Elysium Building. In those days there were only six teams in the National Hockey League, and the Cleveland Barons of the American Hockey League (AHL) were considered by many as the seventh-best team in hockey. Some felt the new arena would open the door for the Barons to join the National Hockey League. The arena sat 9,900 for hockey; 11,000 for basketball; and eventually had crowds of over 14,000 for boxing. Many other events such as the Ice Follies, Knights of Columbus track meets, the Ice Capades, rock concerts, wrestling, car races, the circus, The Harlem Globetrotters, amateur boxing tournaments, and roller derby were also held there. It was an all-purpose arena, and it was rare that some sort of event was not being held.

From December 1937 until November 1973, the arena was the heart of professional boxing in Cleveland. Every major city had a special arena that featured great boxing. In Cleveland, it was the arena at 3717 Euclid Avenue. It truly was the mecca for professional boxing during its tenure.

There were several promoters who tried their hands at featuring fight cards at the Cleveland Arena. When one looks at the glory days of the 1940s and 1950s, the names that stand out are

Bob Brickman and Ben Goetz and eventually Bob Brickman and Larry Atkins. Ed Bang, sports editor of the *Cleveland News*, sponsored an annual Christmas show for 35 years. It was called the Cleveland News Toyshop Fund Boxing Show and was responsible for providing presents for underprivileged youngsters. For the majority of those years, Ed Bang had Larry Atkins as matchmaker, and Atkins not only used most of Cleveland's local talent but also brought in the best fighters the boxing world had to offer. Often his fight cards featured four main events.

In this latest effort of mine, I wanted to show all boxing fans what an amazing boxing city Cleveland once was. Not only did we have a very good crop of local fighters but also promoters like Bob Brickman, Ben Goetz, Larry Atkins, and eventually Don Elbaum, who brought in many of the best fighters from other cities and countries, including many champions. These great fights were held at the Cleveland Arena. Many were featured on televised Friday night and Wednesday night fights, sponsored by Gillette and Pabst Blue Ribbon Beer.

This book offers an overview of 162 fight shows and 903 individual fights that were held at the Cleveland Arena during 1937–1973. Included are many photographs from those events that often featured champions and top contenders from those years.

I hope readers will enjoy and remember what a special time this was in Cleveland boxing history and how special the Cleveland Arena was to this fight town.

One

The 1930s

The Cleveland Arena was built in 1937 for $1.5 million by local sports promoter Albert C. Sutphin and opened for business on November 10, 1937. Promoters and matchmakers such as Bobby Evans, Al Sutphin, Dick Deutsch, Ed Bang, Dan Taylor, and eventually Ben Goetz and Bob Brickman helped launch pro boxing at the arena in late 1937. The first fight show there was on December 6, 1937, the first annual Cleveland News Toyshop Fund Boxing Show.

Because of the late opening there were only a dozen fight shows held at the arena from 1937 through 1939. However, the great Henry Armstrong headlined three times in those first three years. Several local fighters such as former Olympic champion Carmen Barth and other Golden Gloves and national champs also appeared on those dozen cards, along with some well-known local professionals. Those names included Ray Sharkey, Jack Pallat (twice national champion), Mike Gamiere, Frankie Wallace, Eddie Simms, Jesse Levels, Dan Merritt, Paul Pirrone, and future National Boxing Association (NBA) bantamweight champion George Pace.

The Cleveland Arena was off to a great start as a boxing center.

Listed here by date are the first 12 fight shows, including all fighters and ring results, held at the arena to round out the 1930s.

December 6, 1937: Henry Armstrong defended his welterweight title with a first-round technical knockout (TKO) over Tony Chavez, who was knocked down seven times before the fight was stopped at 2:04. On the undercard, Lou Ambers, world lightweight champion, won a 10-round decision over Cleveland's Frankie Wallace. In other bouts, Cleveland's 1932 Olympic Gold Medalist, Carmen Barth, won an eight-round decision over Eric Seelig in a middleweight bout, and Ken Overlin, future middleweight champion, defeated Jack Moran in a six-round decision. In other bouts. Frankie Blair won a six-round decision over Eddie Morgan, and Cleveland's Ray Sharkey won by TKO 5 over Charlie Baxter. Attendance was 12,888 for the annual Cleveland News Toyshop Fund Boxing Show. This was a great start for boxing at the new Cleveland Arena, which had only opened the month before.

January 3, 1938: Cleveland lightweight Ray Sharkey won a 10-round decision over Lloyd Pine of Akron. On the undercard, George Baratko stopped Billy Burke with a TKO in the seventh round, Vito Mangine won a six-round decision over Sammy Taormina (referred to as "Joey Taormina of Akron" in the *Ring* in April 1938, page 64). Ed Murray won by a second-round TKO over Jack Pallat of Cleveland in a battle of heavyweights, and Jimmy White won a four-round decision over Joe Boldin.

March 28, 1938: Cleveland's former Olympic champion, Carmen Barth, won a 10-round split decision over Teddy Yarosz, former middleweight champion. On the undercard, Cleveland's future NBA bantamweight champion, George Pace, won a 10-round decision over Katsumi Morioka; George Baratko won by KO 7 over Babe Dunning, Lou Presto won a six-round decision over Ted Keating, and Hank Pershing lost a four-round decision to Jimmy White.

November 10, 1938: Mike Gamiere, former Cleveland Golden Glove champion, won a 10-round decision over Orville Drouillard. In the co-main event, Henry Hook won a 10-round decision over Pablo Dano. In other bouts, Cleveland's Eddie Simms won a 10-round decision over ? Winston, Vito Mangine won a six-round decision over Joey Wells, and Ralph Veasey won a six-round decision over Jim Brinkman.

November 22, 1938: Mike Gamiere returned and knocked out Kid Sila in the eighth round, Umio Gen won a 10-round decision over Pablo Dano, Eddie Simms won by TKO 5 over Jim McVey, Charley McCarthy won a six-round decision over Ralph Veasey, and Joey Wells won a six-round decision over Vito Mangine.

December 5, 1938: At the annual Cleveland News Toyshop Fund Boxing Show, Henry Armstrong stopped Al Manfredo of Fresno, California, via a third-round TKO in defense of his welterweight championship. The time was 1:45 when referee Tony LaBranch stopped the contest. On the undercard, Lou Ambers defeated Frankie Wallace again, this time with a sixth-round TKO. The time when referee Benny Leonard stopped the contest was 3:00. In other bouts, Solly Krieger, NBA middleweight champion, won a 10-round decision over Carmen Barth, and Petey Sarron, former featherweight champion, won a 10-round decision over Clevelander Mike Gamiere. In two other prelim bouts, Tiger Jackson won a four-round decision over Eddie Morgan, and Dan Merritt won by TKO 2 over Jack Gross, who was making his debut. The time of the bout was 2:51. The referee was Lou Parker, and attendance was 12,784.

December 20, 1938: In a battle of Cleveland heavyweights, Eddie Simms won by TKO 8 over Lem Franklin. On the undercard, Umio Gen lost a 10-round decision to Henry Hook, Johnny "Bandit" Romero stopped Irving Pease in the first round by TKO, Pablo Dano won a 10-round decision over Cleveland's Jesse Levels, Dan Merritt stopped Harry Feuerstein by a KO in round one, and Horace Gresham won by third round kayo over Charley McCarthy.

January 16, 1939: Marty Simmons stopped Johnny "Bandit" Romero in the eighth round by TKO because of a badly cut mouth. Eddie Simms won a 10-round split decision over Eddie Blunt, Pablo Dano won a 10-round decision over Cleveland's Olympian Lou Laurie, and Clinton Bridges was knocked out in the first round by Willie Muldune of Cleveland. The final bout saw Dan Merritt winning by a TKO 2 over George Cerosky. Bobby Evans was the promoter.

February 23, 1939: Johnny Whiters won by a KO in sixth round over Buff Mellinger. Cleveland's Willie Muldune won an eight-round unanimous decision over Johnny "Bandit" Romero, Dan Merritt stopped Ted Keating in the opening round, Cleveland's Mike Minnich won a six-round decision over Mickey Breen, and Horace Gresham won by a KO 2 over John Skelly.

March 1, 1939: George Pace, Cleveland's bantamweight contender, won a 10-round decision over Henry Hook. The NBA had ordered world champion Sixto Escobar to defend his title against the winner of this fight, but Escobar relinquished the title. On October 29, the NBA proclaimed George Pace champion. Pablo Dano won an eight-round split decision over Lou Laurie, and Johnny "Bandit" Romero won by a TKO 2 over Eddie Moran. The time was 1:47 when referee Tony LaBranch stopped the contest. Cleveland's Lee Sheppard won by a second-round TKO over Larry Cisneros. The time was 1:53 when referee Matt Brock halted the fight. Ed Murray won a four-round decision over Chuck Belair, who was making his debut.

March 7, 1939: Marty Simmons won a 10-round decision over Paulie Sykes. In a battle of Cleveland heavyweights, Eddie Simms won a 10-round decision over Dan Merritt, Johnny "Bandit" Romero won by an eight-round decision over Willie Muldune, and Tiger Brown won by a TKO 1 over Horace Gresham.

December 11, 1939: At the Cleveland News Toyshop Fund Boxing Show, Henry Armstrong headlined and made it three straight wins as he stopped Jimmy Garrison of Kansas City in the seventh round, in defense of his welterweight title. The time was 1:19 when referee Benny Leonard ended the contest. In the 10-round cofeature, Al Hostak, NBA middleweight champion, defended his title with a stunning first-round kayo of Eric Seelig of Germany. The time was 1:21 when referee Tony LaBranch called a halt to the match. Billy Soose, future world middleweight champion, edged Cleveland's Paul Pirrone via a six-round decision. The referee was Joe Sedley. In other bouts, Dave Castilloux won a six-round decision over Mike Gamiere, Milo Theodorescu won a six-round decision over Leonard Bennett, and Cleveland's Jimmy Reeves stopped Horace Gresham in the first round. The time was 1:21.

Seen here is the groundbreaking for Cleveland Arena on May 16, 1937. Al Sutphin and Cleveland officials break ground for the new arena at 3717 Euclid Avenue. (Courtesy of Clevelandscene.com)

The exterior of the Cleveland Arena is pictured a decade after the groundbreaking, during its professional boxing heyday. (Courtesy of Encyclopedia of Cleveland History / Case Western Reserve University.)

Born in Italy, Frankie "Chee Chee" Wallace fought many greats, including several champions. He was world rated in two different divisions—featherweight and lightweight—during his career despite losing more than he won from 1930 to 1941. He fought twice at the arena, including the very first show on December 6, 1937, losing to world lightweight champion Lou Ambers.

Carmen Barth was a local Golden Gloves champion who won the Olympic gold medal as a middleweight at the 1932 games in Los Angeles. As a professional, Carmen fought from 1932 to 1941. He met Freddie Steele for the NBA middleweight title, losing by a seventh-round TKO on February 19, 1939, at Cleveland Public Hall. His arena bouts included appearing in two of the first three shows in 1937–1938, defeating Eric Seelig and losing to Solly Krieger.

Mike Gamiere was a local Golden Gloves champion who won the National Golden Gloves in 1935 in the lightweight division. As a professional, from 1936 to 1946, he had 52 fights and fought on arena cards six times.

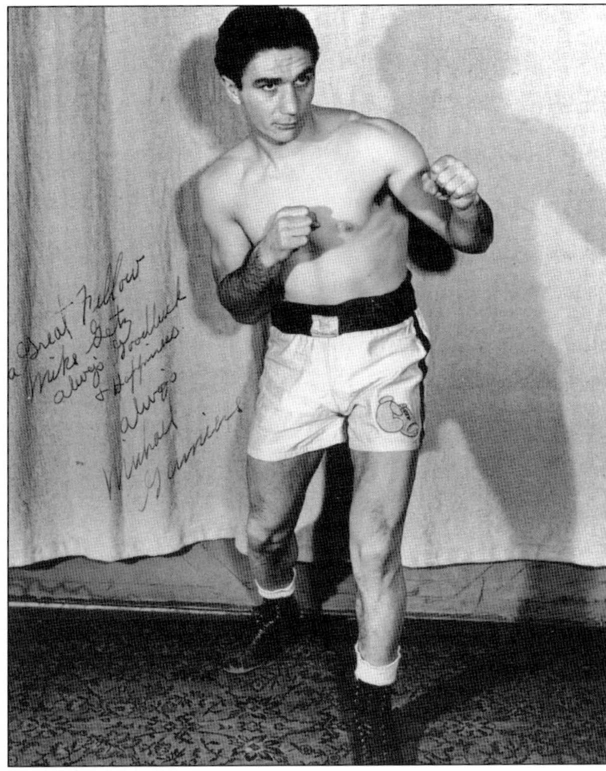

Eddie Simms was a colorful Cleveland heavyweight who fought five times in the early days of the arena, between 1938 and 1939. His overall career record from 1930 through 1949 was not great, losing as many as he won, but he did have career victories over Tony Musto, Jack Roper, Buddy Scott, and Al Ettore and two wins over fellow Clevelander Lem Franklin. (Photograph by H.A. Attwell Studio, Chicago.)

George Pace was a Cleveland Golden Gloves champion in 1933. As a professional bantamweight, he became the NBA world champion on November 2, 1939. Pace fought at the arena twice, in 1938 and again in 1939, defeating Katsumi Morioka and Henry Hook.

Paul Pirrone was a Cleveland boxer who fought in several weight divisions and was a top-rated middleweight in the mid-1930s. He lost his one fight at the arena, a sixth-round decision to Billy Soose on December 11, 1939, on the Cleveland News Toyshop Fund Boxing Show.

Al Hostak, the Seattle-based former NBA middleweight champion, appeared in Cleveland only one time. On December 11, 1939, at the third annual Cleveland News Toyshop Fund Boxing Show, held at the new Cleveland Arena, he shocked German challenger Eric Seelig by stopping him in the first round in defense of his championship.

Henry Armstrong, considered by most experts as one of the top five fighters of all time, fought on the first three Cleveland News Toyshop Fund Boxing Shows at the then new Cleveland Arena, from 1937 to 1939. He successfully defended his welterweight title each time.

Henry Armstrong (right) jabs challenger Jimmy Garrison at the December 11, 1939, Cleveland News Toyshop Fund Boxing Show. Armstrong successfully defended his world welterweight title with a technical knockout when referee Benny Leonard, former lightweight champion, halted the contest at 1:19 of the seventh round.

Two

1940–1944

Without a doubt, the 1940s were the glory years of professional boxing at the Cleveland Arena. Starting on October 22, 1940, and continuing through December 19, 1944, there were 34 fight shows held.

Promoters and matchmakers such as Bobby Evans, Al Sutphin, Dick Deutsch, Ed Bang, and Dan Taylor, and eventually Ben Goetz and Bob Brickman helped boxing take off. When Larry Atkins joined the team, fans were treated to even more amazing shows.

Bob Brickman and Larry Atkins eventually worked as a team to put Cleveland on the boxing map, competing with other bigtime boxing cities such as New York, Chicago, and Pittsburgh, and holding their own.

Local stars such as Jimmy Bivins, Joey Maxim, Chuck Hunter, Lem Franklin, Lloyd Marshall, and Jimmy Reeves, to name just a few, entered the professional ranks and made a big impact on the arena fight shows in those early years. Chuck Hunter and Jimmy Bivins appeared 28 and 23 times respectively, the most of any fighters.

Many of the all-time fight crowds and gates took place during the years 1940–1944, most of them on Ed Bang's Cleveland News Toyshop Fund Shows, but others also drew large crowds. It was a boom time for the Cleveland Arena.

Listed here in order are all arena fight cards, contenders, and results from those first five years of the 1940s.

October 22, 1940: Jimmy Bivins, a product of the Cleveland Golden Gloves, had his first Cleveland Arena showing as a middleweight and won a 10-round decision over Vince Pimpinella to run his record to 18-0. On the same card, Anton Christoforidis defeated Cleveland National Amateur Athletic Union (AAU) champion Jimmy Reeves by a second-round kayo, and Tommy Yarosz won a five-round decision over Juan Tomaz. Cleveland middleweight Bobby Berry defeated Ralph Veasey by a third round TKO. In another bout, Benny Calla won by a TKO 2 over Joe Berger. The time was 3:00 when referee Joe Sedley stopped the contest. In the last fight local lightweight Max Schindler won his debut by a four-round decision over Tony Lanese, also a local fighter. Bob Brickman was the promoter.

December 2, 1940: Jimmy Bivins fought on his first Cleveland News Toyshop Fund Boxing Show and was defeated by Anton Christoforidis by a majority 10-round decision. Christoforidis was floored for a nine count in the second round but came on strong to win the decision. Bivins weighed 159.5 pounds and Christoforidis was 163. It was Jimmy Bivins's first defeat after going 19-0 to begin his professional career. On the undercard, South American heavyweight Arturo Godoy won a 10-round decision over roly-poly Tony Musto in what was described as a savage heavyweight brawl. Mike Kaplan defeated Saverio Turiello in a 10-round decision; Pat Comiskey knocked out Don Siegel in the first round; and in a battle of former Cleveland Golden Glove champions, Mike Gamiere decisioned former National AAU champion Georgie Toy over eight rounds. And Everett Rightmire won a six-round decision over Mike Raffa. Attendance was 12,000 with a gate of $30,000.

January 13, 1941: Anton Christoforidis defeated Melio Bettina by a 15-round unanimous decision to win the NBA light-heavyweight title. Chief Crazy Horse defeated Cleveland's Lee Sheppard by a six-round decision; Jimmy Reeves, a Cleveland Golden Gloves champion, bested Willie Pavlovich by a TKO in the fourth round; and Joey Maxim, Cleveland National AAU and National Golden Gloves champion (1940) made his pro debut by winning a four-round decision over a fellow Clevelander, Bobby Berry. In other bouts, Beauford Glover won his debut with a TKO 2 over Juan Tomaz, and Joey Speer won a four-round decision over Don Blatchford.

March 5, 1941: Jimmy Bivins won a 10-round decision over former middleweight kingpin Teddy Yarosz, knocking him down in the eighth round. Maxie Berger won by a TKO 7 over Cleveland's Mike Gamiere, Joey Pirrone won by TKO 5 over Max Schindler, and Bobby Berry won a five-round decision over Billy Burke. In two other five-round bouts, Steve Morgan won over Steve Kulich and Beauford Glover defeated Erwin Hicks, both bouts by decision.

April 29, 1941: Lenny Mancini won a 10-round split decision over Billy Marquart. Maxie Berger won a 10-round decision over Pete DeRuzza. Joey Maxim defeated Cleveland rival Bobby Berry by decision for a second time, this time in a six-round bout. Jimmy Reeves won by a TKO in the first round over Al Reiss. Pete Spotti won a six-round unanimous decision over Cleveland National AAU champion Georgie Toy in a welterweight match, and Sammy Secreet decisioned Beauford Glover in a five-round bout.

September 10, 1941: Jimmy Bivins lost a 10-round split decision to Tony Musto. Bivins, despite giving away 26 pounds, had Musto on the deck in the first round. Maxie Berger lost a 10-round decision to Sammy Secreet of Pittsburgh. Tommy Yarosz won a five-round decision over Oakie Greer, Cleveland's Harry Teaney won by a fourth-round kayo over Johnny Ryan, Bobby Berry won a five-round unanimous decision over Steve Morgan, and Pat Murphy won a five-round decision over Goff Greer.

September 24, 1941: In one of the wildest fights ever in Cleveland, Jimmy Reeves pounded future middleweight champion Jake LaMotta all over the ring for the early part of their bout before running out of gas. In round nine, Reeves went through the ropes for a nine count. In the 10th, he went down four times—twice from punches and twice from pure exhaustion. The referee Joe Sedley felt Reeves had piled up enough points to win if he was not counted out. When the bout ended, he was on the floor. The final tally was a split decision win for Reeves, and the fans went crazy and a riot broke out. Fans booed for 20 minutes. On the undercard, Cleveland heavyweight Lem Franklin knocked Tony Musto into submission in the second round, Mimmie Adragna decisioned Joey Wells in a five-round contest, Harry Teaney won a five-round decision over Sammy Adragna, and Sammy Secreet knocked out Mitsos Grispos in the second round.

October 20, 1941: Jimmy Reeves and Jake LaMotta were rematched, and it was almost a repeat performance by Reeves as he piled up an insurmountable lead for the first eight rounds. It was a slugfest the rest of the way, but Reeves won by unanimous decision. Cleveland's heavyweight hopeful, Lem Franklin, at 201 pounds, defeated Big Abe Simon, weighing 255 pounds via a TKO in five rounds. The time was 1:33 when referee Joe Sedley stopped the contest. Simon had been down in the first, second, fourth, and fifth rounds before the ending. Franklin suffered a broken hand. Maxie Berger lost by a split decision in 10 rounds against Sammy Secreet, Jackie Adragna won a five-round decision over Willie Cutsinger, Harry Teaney won by a TKO 4 over Al Sayres, and Jack Stauffer won a five-round decision over Johnny Williams. Attendance was 13,256 with a gate of $31,623.80. The promoters were Bob Brickman and Benny Goetz.

November 17, 1941: Jimmy Bivins lost a 10-round unanimous decision against Melio Bettina. Jackie Wilson, known as "California" Jackie Wilson, won a 10-round unanimous decision over Sammy Secreet. Maxie Berger won a 10-round decision over Beauford Glover, Cleveland's Harry Teaney dropped a five-round decision against Billy Murray, Jackie Adragna won a five-round decision over Willie Cutsinger, and Jackie Stauffer won a five-round decision over Eddie Watkins.

December 1, 1941: Anton Christoforidis won a hard-fought 10-round decision over former middleweight champion Ceferino Garcia on the Cleveland News Toyshop Fund Boxing Show. Fritzie Zivic stopped Harry Weekly via a TKO in the ninth round, and Joey Maxim had his first major bout as he trounced Red Burman to win a 10-round decision. Joey Pirrone, brother of Paul Pirrone, won a six-round decision over K.O. Borrado. In other bouts, Johnny Lawer, local welterweight, won his ring debut by a TKO 3 over Don Blatchford, and Johnny Abbott, Cleveland welterweight, won a four-round decision over Henry Claypool. Attendance was approximately 12,000 with a gate of $35,000.

December 18, 1941: "California" Jackie Wilson won by a third-round TKO over Mike Kaplan. Billy Soose won a 10-round decision over Jimmy Reeves, Garvey Young won by an eight-round decision over Victor Troise, and Harvey Dubbs won a five-round split decision over Billy Murray. Also on the undercard, Jimmy Grimm won a five-round decision over Mike Lucas, and Gib Jones won by a third-round KO over Jackie Stauffer.

January 13, 1942: Jimmy Bivins won a 10-round unanimous decision over former middleweight champion Billy Soose. "California" Jackie Wilson won a 10-round decision over Quentin Breese, Sammy Secreet won an eight-round decision over Tony Ferrara, Bobby Berry defeated Gib Jones in a five-rounder, and Henry Claypool bested Cleveland's Johnny Abbott in five rounds.

February 24, 1942: Bob Pastor won by an eighth-round knockout over Lem Franklin; the time was 2:08. Billy Marquart won an eight-round decision over Tony Ferrara, and Joe Muscato won by a KO 2 over Bill Petersen. The time for that match was 1:32. In other bouts, Garvey Young won by a TKO 3 over Victor Troise with a time of 1:22 when referee Lou Parker stopped the contest.

Johnny Lawer won a five-round decision over Ernie Pelaia, and Billy Murray won a five-round unanimous decision over Charley Eschman. This card set an indoor record at the time with 13,278 fans paying out $52,444. The promoters were Benny Goetz and Bob Brickman.

March 11, 1942: Jimmy Bivins won a 10-round unanimous decision over reigning light-heavy champion Gus Lesnevich in a nontitle match, knocking down Lesnevich in the second round. Joey Maxim knocked out Herbie Katz in the sixth round with a time of 1:06. In other bouts, Tommy Yarosz lost a five-round decision to Clevelander Johnny Lawer, Joe Muscato knocked out Charley Roth in the second round by a TKO, Curley Denton won a five-round split decision over Henry Claypool, and Tom Glaspy won a four-round decision over Eddie Morgan.

April 17, 1942: Jimmy Bivins had Bob Pastor on the deck twice in the first round but let him slip away and lost a 10-round split decision. Anton Christoforidis won a 10-round decision over Jimmy Reeves in a battle of local light-heavyweights. Joe Muscato, a Buffalo heavyweight, returned and scored a first-round kayo over Jack Savage; Gib Jones lost a five-round decision to Johnny Lawer; and Gus Mullner, former Golden Gloves champion, knocked out Jack Kelly in his ring debut in a heavyweight match. The time was 2:41. A total of 12,472 fans paid $47,026 to see the matches that night.

July 23, 1942: Jimmy Bivins knocked out previously undefeated Joe Muscato in the fifth round; the time was 0:57. Harry Teaney lost an eight-rounder to Billy Murray, and Phil Muscato won a rare seven-round decision over Johnny Lawer. In a series of five-round bouts, Harold Dettman lost by decision to Charley Hayes, and Bobby Richardson stopped Billy Seep by a TKO in the first round, and the time was 1:18. Sammy Derrico won a decision over Freddie Bernhardt in his ring debut.

September 15, 1942: Jimmy Bivins knocked down Tami Mauriello in the first round and won a 10-round split decision. Jimmy Reeves won an eight-round decision over Phil Muscato; Sonny Horne won by decision over Jimmy Mandell in an eight-rounder; Bobby Richardson won by a TKO in third round over Johnny Baldesino; and Buddy Smallwood, in his ring debut, won a four-round decision over Jimmy Trusso.

October 20, 1942: Jimmy Bivins won a 10-round split decision over Bob Pastor in a rematch. Scoring was 7-2-1 and 6-3-1 for Bivins and 5-4-1 for Pastor. Vince Dell'Orto stopped Harry Teaney by a TKO in the fourth. Teaney had a bad cut over his right eye, which appeared to have happened from a headbutt. Frankie Best won his debut by a five-round decision over Johnny Lawer, Bobby Berger lost on points in a five-round fight to Bobby Richardson, and Jimmy Trusso won a five-round decision over Jue Yee Kong.

December 1, 1942: The annual Cleveland News Toyshop Fund Boxing Show featured Ezzard Charles winning a 10-round unanimous decision over Joey Maxim. In the co-main event, Sugar Ray Robinson won by a TKO 8 over Izzy Jannazzo, Harry Bobo knocked out Larry Lane in the first round, Maxie Berger won an eight-round unanimous decision over Bobby Richardson, and Joey Pirrone won by a TKO 1 over Dick Cramer. Attendance was 12,190 with a gate of $47,934.

December 22, 1942: Anton Christoforidis won a 10-round unanimous decision over Nate Bolden. On the undercard, Lulu Costantino won an eight-round split decision over Joey Pirrone, Maxie Berger won an eight-round decision over Bobby Richardson, Jimmy Reeves won a six-round decision over Frankie Best, and Bobby McQuillar won by a KO 2 over Sammy Scully.

January 7, 1943: Jimmy Bivins completely dominated Ezzard Charles, flooring him four times (some sources said more) and winning a 10-round unanimous decision. This was in the finals of the Duration Light-heavyweight Tournament. Joey Archibald, former featherweight champion, lost an eight-round unanimous decision to Cleveland's Joey Pirrone; Bobby Richardson knocked out Jimmy Willis in the second round; Johnny Lawer bested Curley Denton in a six-round match; and Bobby McQuillar won a six-round decision over Abie Kaufman.

February 23, 1943: Jimmy Bivins won the Duration Light-heavyweight Tournament title with a 15-round unanimous decision over Anton Christoforidis. Izzy Jannazzo won a 10-round decision over Bobby Richardson, Ike Williams knocked out Bobby McQuillar in the third round, Abe Denner lost on points in six to Angel Aviles, and Jackie Armitage won a five-round decision over Berry Wright.

March 10, 1943: Joey Maxim was stunned by a first-round knockout against Curtis Sheppard. It was his only knockout loss as a pro. The time was 0:51, and the referee Joe Sedley. Chalky Wright, former featherweight champion, won by a third-round kayo over Joey Pirrone, and Henry Vasquez won by a TKO in the third round over Jose Aponte Torres. Referee Vito Mazzeo stopped the fight at 0:44 of the round because of a badly cut right eye. Hilton "Fitzie" Fitzpatrick won by a second-round KO over Jack McCahill; the time was 0:24. Jackie Armitage won a five-round decision over Joey Ross.

March 31, 1943: Lloyd Marshall completely dominated Ezzard Charles, knocking him down eight times before the referee stopped the fight in the eighth round. Charles did not win a single round. The time was 0:25 when referee Jackie Davis stopped the contest. In other bouts, Joey Maxim got back in the ring with Curtis Sheppard just three weeks after suffering his knockout defeat and won a 10-round unanimous decision, winning 9 out of 10 rounds. Sammy Secreet lost by a TKO in the eighth round against Izzy Jannazzo because of a badly cut right eye. Alex Doyle lost by a TKO in the fourth round against Bobby McQuillar, and Hilton "Fitzie" Fitzpatrick won a five-round decision over Curley Denton. Attendance was 10,539.

April 21, 1943: Lloyd Marshall gave Anton Christoforidis a pasting as he won a 10-round unanimous decision over the former NBA light-heavy king. Heavyweight Buddy Walker bested Patsy Perroni over eight rounds, Ray Brown won by a TKO in the fifth round over Alvin Gomez, and Ike Williams scored a fourth-round TKO over Joe Genovese. The time was 2:57, and the referee was Joe Sedley. Fitzie Fitzpatrick won a five-round decision over Rocky Luciano.

October 22, 1943: Lee Savold kayoed Eddie Blunt in round one. The time was 1:02, and the referee was Joe Sedley. In other bouts, Jackie Wilson, former NBA featherweight champion, lost a 10-round split decision to Freddie Pope; Fitzie Fitzpatrick won a six-round decision over Bill McDowell; Chuck Hunter won by a KO 2 over Bobby Maloney; and Juste Fontaine won a four-round decision over Leroy Jackson.

December 1, 1943: The Cleveland News Toyshop Fund Boxing Show featured Jimmy Bivins winning a 10-round unanimous decision over Lee Q Murray. Scoring was 4-3-3, 5-3-2, 5-3-2. Joey Maxim won by a TKO in the sixth round over Claudio Villar, who was knocked down four times. Lulu Constantino won by a TKO in the fourth round over Freddie Pope, Chuck Hunter lost to Maxie Berger by eight-round unanimous decision, Fitzie Fitzpatrick won an eight-round decision over Sammy Kirsch, and Berry Wright decisioned Lee Hogan in four. A record crowd of 14,500 with a gate total of $56,000 watched the matches at the annual show.

January 18, 1944: Lloyd Marshall defeated Nate Bolden by a 10-round unanimous decision. Some reports said this was for the vacant Duration world light-heavyweight title, but not much was ever made of that. Maxie Berger knocked out Pete Galiano in the second round with a time of 0:25. In other bouts, Fitzie Fitzpatrick lost by a TKO in round six to Len Wadsworth, Johnny Lawer scored a big win by knocking out fellow Clevelander Jimmy Reeves in 1:05 of the second round, and Chuck Hunter won by a TKO in the fourth round over Don Eddy.

February 29, 1944: Jimmy Bivins defeated Lee Q. Murray again by a 10-round decision before another large crowd of 13,774. The gate total was $61,496. Phil Muscato won by a sixth-round TKO over Jimmy Brown, and Lee Oma won on a fourth-round TKO over Johnny Denson. The time was 2:46, and the referee was Jackie Davis. In other bouts, Johnny Allen knocked out Charley Roth in the third round, Berry Wright won by a TKO in the third round over Erwin Hicks, and Tony Brush won a four-round split decision over Jackie Gaines. Both Brush and Gaines were making their pro debuts.

March 22, 1944: Tommy Bell won by a KO 1 over Maxie Berger as Berger suffered a broken ankle when knocked down. The time was 2:27. On the undercard, Mayon Padlo won an eight-round split decision over Berry Wright, and Fitzie Fitzpatrick won by a KO 1 over Phil Muscato with a time of 0:57. In other bouts, Chuck Hunter scored a second-round TKO over Jess Glenn, and Youngstown's Tony Janiro won by a TKO 3 over Cisco Diaz, who was making his debut.

April 21, 1944: Lloyd Marshall won easily over Jake LaMotta in a 10-round unanimous decision. In other bouts, Fitzie Fitzpatrick won a 10-round decision over Johnny Finazzo, Johnny Ryan bested Jackie Gaines in six rounds, and Clevelander Leroy Jackson decisioned Mike Martyk also in six rounds. Another Cleveland product, middleweight Sampson Powell, won by a TKO in the third round over Rudy Zorich with a time of 1:54. The referee was Lou Parker. Heavyweight Walter Thomas won a six-round decision over Dave Mason, who was making his ring debut.

October 18, 1944: Lloyd Marshall won a 10-round split decision over Joe Carter. On the undercard, Chuck Hunter won by a referee technical decision (RTD) in the third round when his opponent Freddie Archer could not answer the bell for the fourth round. Johnny Flynn knocked out Gilbert Stromquist in the opening round, Lou Dell lost a decision to Mike Martyk in a six-rounder, Bob Blevins lost a unanimous decision to Gus Mullner in five rounds, and Clevelander Tony Brush bested Herman Pope in another five-round contest.

December 5, 1944: At the Cleveland News Toyshop Fund Boxing Show, Willie Pep won a 10-round unanimous decision over Chalky Wright. On the undercard, Ike Williams won a 10-round unanimous decision over Lulu Constantino, Johnny Flynn won by a KO 1 over Frank Androff, Cleveland's Leroy Jackson stopped Lou Dell by a fourth-round TKO, and Bob Blevins won a five-round decision over Gus Mullner. Gate receipts set a record for the time at $74,641.

December 19, 1944: Tommy Bell won a 10-round unanimous decision over Chuck Hunter, and Johnny Flynn won a 10-round split decision over Joey Maxim in the co-main event. Bob Blevins won by a TKO 4 over Gene Finks, Tony Brush won a five-round unanimous decision over Art Brown, and Stanley Myka won by a TKO in the third round over Frankie Perroni.

Saverio Turiello falls outside of the ropes against Mike Kaplan on December 2, 1940. Kaplan won a 10-round decision at the Cleveland News Toyshop Fund Boxing Show. (Photograph by Eddie Dork.)

Tony Musto was a heavyweight who fought from 1937 to 1946. He defeated Johnny Risko by knockout in 1940, in Risko's last fight. At the arena, Musto had victories over Buddy Knox, Jimmy Bivins, and Lem Franklin, all in 1941.

Anton Christoforidis, the Greek fighter who made Cleveland his home during the 1940s, had some excellent fights here, including an exciting three-bout series with Cleveland rival Jimmy Bivins. The highlight of his time in Cleveland was winning the vacant NBA light-heavyweight championship over southpaw Melio Bettina. Anton displays his championship belt in this photograph.

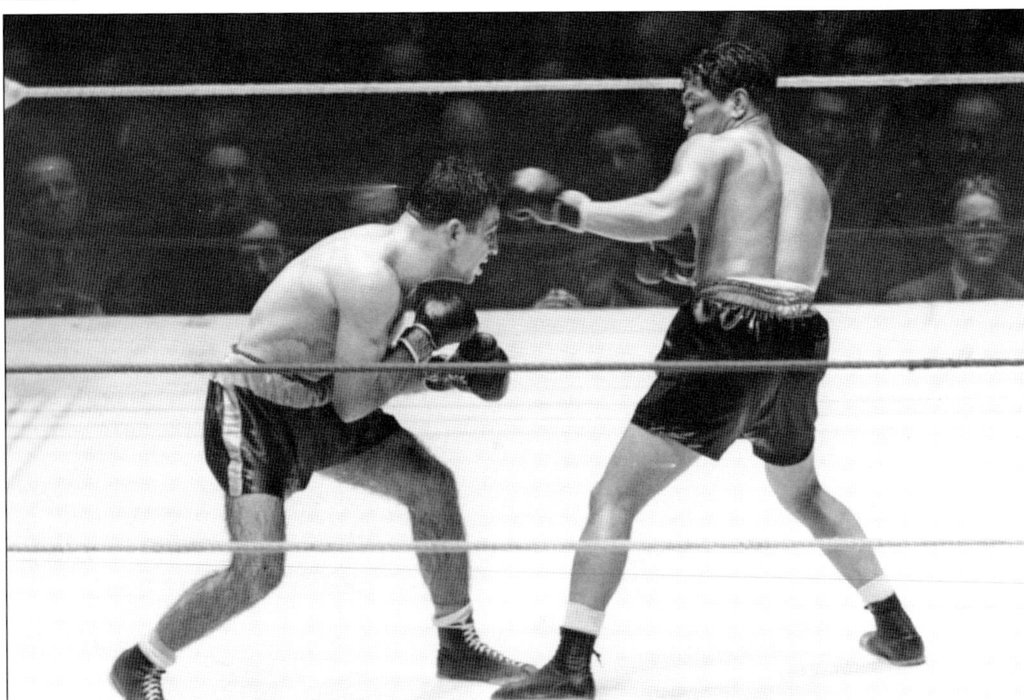

Anton Christoforidis (left) and Ceferino Garcia (right) are pictured in action on December 1, 1941. Christoforidis won a hard-fought decision over the former middleweight champion at the annual Cleveland News Toyshop Fund Boxing Show.

Anton Christoforidis (left) and Melio Bettina (right) battle it out for the vacant NBA light-heavyweight title on January 13, 1941, at the arena. Christoforidis prevailed with a 15-round unanimous decision.

Melio Bettina fought at the Cleveland Arena on January 13, 1941, losing in his bid to win the vacant NBA light-heavyweight title against Anton Christoforidis by a 15-round unanimous decision. Bettina returned to the arena and won a 10-round unanimous decision over Jimmy Bivins on November 17, 1941.

Jake LaMotta was not only famous for being a world middleweight champion but also for his six-bout series with Sugar Ray Robinson. LaMotta did not have a lot of success in Cleveland, however, losing twice to Jimmy Reeves and once to Lloyd Marshall in the 1940s before defeating Chuck Hunter in 1950.

Cleveland's Jimmy Reeves hangs on after getting knocked through the ropes in the ninth round in his first fight with Jake LaMotta on September 24, 1941. Reeves barely survived to win this 10-round decision at the Cleveland Arena. (Photograph by Glenn Zahn.)

Abe Simon was a 255-pound heavyweight who knocked out Jersey Joe Walcott and fought heavyweight champion Joe Louis twice for the title. Simon only fought at the Cleveland Arena once, at the end of his career, and was stopped by a technical knockout in the fifth round by local heavyweight star Lem Franklin on October 20, 1941.

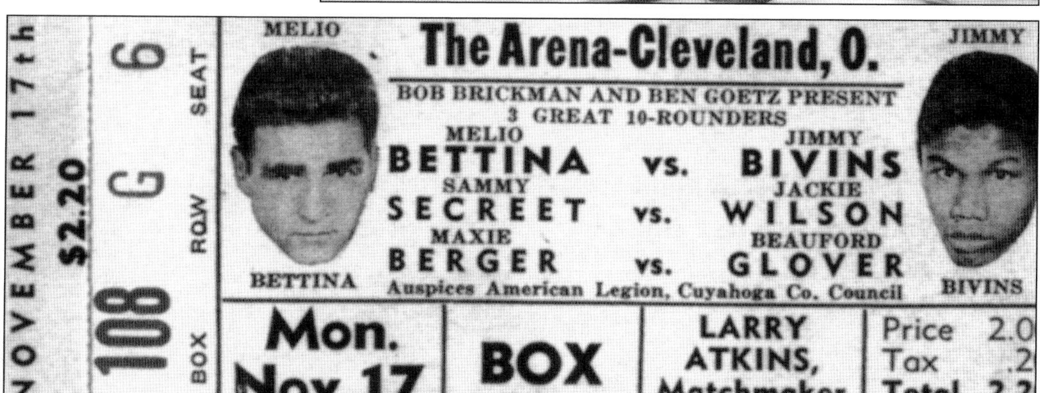

Here is the Jimmy Bivins and Melio Bettina ticket for their November 17, 1941, fight. Bettina won by unanimous decision.

Harry Teaney was a Cleveland lightweight who fought from 1939 to 1949. Teaney fought in many places and met some of the best, including Tippy Larkin, Freddie Dawson, Fritzie Zivic, and Lulu Costantino. In 1941 and 1942, Teaney fought five bouts at the Cleveland Arena.

Ceferino Garcia, former world middleweight champion, fought only one time in Cleveland, losing a rousing 10-round decision to Anton Christoforidis at the Cleveland News Toyshop Fund Boxing Show on December 1, 1941.

Hilton "Fitzie" Fitzpatrick was a West Virginia light-heavy whose career lasted from 1941 to 1953. Fitzie, who was legally deaf, fought at the Cleveland Arena nine different times during the 1940s.

Harry Weekly is down for the first time in the seventh round against Fritzie Zivic at the December 1, 1941, Cleveland News Toyshop Fund Boxing Show. Zivic would go on to stop Weekly by a TKO at 2:57 in the ninth round of their welterweight match.

Clevelander Joey Pirrone and K.O. Borrado get tangled up in the second round of their December 1, 1941, bout at the Cleveland News Toyshop Fund Boxing Show. Pirrone won a six-round decision.

Billy Soose, former world middleweight champion, fought twice at the Cleveland Arena, winning his first bout by a 10-round decision over Clevelander Jimmy Reeves on December 18, 1941, then losing a unanimous decision to Jimmy Bivins on January 13, 1942. Shortly after the Bivins bout, Soose retired.

Jimmy Bivins was without a doubt one of the greatest fighters to ever come out of Cleveland. Besides being a two-time Golden Gloves champion and runner-up in the 1939 AAU as a welterweight, his pro career from 1940 to 1955 saw him ranked number one in both the light-heavyweight and heavyweight divisions at the same time. His 86 career wins included defeating eight world champs and countless other contenders.

Billy Soose (left) and Jimmy Bivins (right) are seen in action on January 13, 1942. Bivins won a 10-round unanimous decision against the former middleweight champion. After this contest, Soose decided to retire for good. (Photograph by Jerry Horton.)

Tami Mauriello was a heavyweight contender from Bronx, New York, who fought Jimmy Bivins twice—once in Cleveland and once in New York. In their Cleveland Arena fight on September 15, 1942, Bivins won a 10-round split decision.

Jimmy Bivins takes it to world light-heavyweight champion Gus Lesnevich in route to a 10-round unanimous decision. Bivins floored Lesnevich in the second round and won an easy decision in their nontitle fight on March 11, 1942.

Jimmy Bivins floors Ezzard Charles on January 7, 1943. Bivins knocked down the future heavyweight champion four times and won a 10-round unanimous decision in the semifinal bout of the wartime or "duration" light-heavyweight championship.

Lem Franklin was a local Golden Gloves champion in 1936 and became a heavyweight contender who fought at the arena four times between 1938 and 1942. Tragically, Franklin was knocked out in the ninth round by Larry Lane in New Jersey on July 24, 1944, suffering a serious brain injury. He died on August 3, 1944.

Local heavyweight Lem Franklin is on the attack against Bob Pastor on February 24, 1942. In the battle of heavyweight contenders, Pastor stopped Franklin at the 2:08 mark in the eighth round.

Bobby Berry, a Cleveland middleweight, fought seven times at the arena. He was Joey Maxim's first professional opponent and met some very good fighters during his career from 1940 to 1949.

Bob Pastor was a heavyweight contender who met Joe Louis for the world title in 1939, losing by an 11th-round knockout. He fought three times at the arena between 1940 and 1942, splitting decisions with Jimmy Bivins and knocking out Lem Franklin. After losing a split decision to Jimmy Bivins in their second bout on October 20, 1942, Pastor retired.

Joey Archibald, former world featherweight champion in the 1940s, fought once at the arena, losing to Joey Pirrone by an eight-round unanimous decision on January 7, 1943.

Curtis Sheppard, known as "Hatchetman," was a powerful punching light-heavyweight who was the only fighter to ever knock out Cleveland's Joey Maxim in the pro ranks. He accomplished that feat at the arena on March 10, 1943, in the first round.

Cleveland Arena hosts a capacity crowd in this 1943 photograph. (Courtesy of the Michael Schwartz Library, Cleveland State University.)

Patsy Perroni was a Canton, Ohio, heavyweight contender who had a lengthy career from 1927 to 1944. He defeated Cleveland's Johnny Risko three times and met Joe Louis and many other excellent fighters. In his only arena appearance on April 21, 1943, he lost to Buddy Walker by a six-round decision.

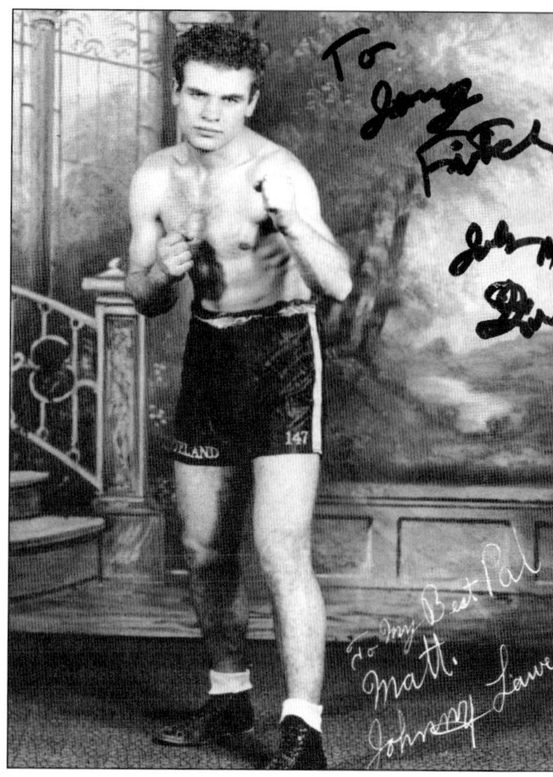

Johnny Lawer was a Cleveland middleweight who fought from 1941 to 1947. He fought in arena fight shows nine times, with his biggest win being an upset victory over fellow Clevelander Jimmy Reeves, who he knocked out at 1:05 of the second round on January 18, 1944.

Albert "Chalky" Wright, former world featherweight champion, fought twice at the Cleveland Arena, knocking out Joey Pirrone in the third round on March 10, 1943, and losing a 10-round unanimous decision to Willie Pep at the Cleveland News Toyshop Fund Boxing Show on December 5, 1944.

Georgie Toy was a local Golden Gloves champion who went on to win the National AAU in 1939 as a lightweight. Toy only had 13 professional fights with a 9-4 record, and he appeared on arena cards four times from 1941 to 1946.

Lloyd Marshall won the Cleveland Golden Gloves as a middleweight in 1934 and 1935. His amateur record is listed as 212-7. As a professional, from 1936 to 1951, he was ranked as the top contender in the light-heavyweight division and defeated 9 of 12 world champions.

Lloyd Marshall, light-heavyweight contender, batters Nate Bolden along the ropes as he wins a 10-round decision on January 18, 1944, one of his five appearances at the arena. He had moved from Cleveland to California in 1936.

Ike Williams was one of 50 champions who appeared at the Cleveland Arena from 1937 to 1973. Williams was considered one of the top lightweight champions in modern boxing history. He fought in Cleveland four times in the 1940s with all bouts ending in victory for Williams.

Lee Q. Murray was a hard-punching heavyweight from Connecticut who fought Jimmy Bivins five times, including three at the Cleveland Arena in the 1940s.

Willie Pep was a two-time world featherweight champion who appeared once at the arena. On December 5, 1944, at the Cleveland News Toyshop Fund Boxing Show, he defeated former champion Chalky Wright by a 10-round decision.

Leroy Jackson was a Cleveland lightweight who had 40 professional fights during his short career from 1943 to 1946. He had mixed results but was very popular, appearing at the arena 14 times.

Three

1945–1949

The first five years of the 1940s were very successful for local boxing, and this continued on throughout the decade. With the team of Bob Brickman and Larry Atkins promoting and with World War II ending, the fight scene continued to thrive.

From 1945 to 1949, the arena hosted 46 shows. By the time the 1940s were over, there had been a total of 441 individual fights held at the Cleveland Arena. This was the greatest decade in the history of the venue.

Larry Atkins was a highly respected man in fight circles, not only in Cleveland but also in New York and elsewhere. Atkins had started in boxing on Jack Dempsey's team, and apparently fighters and their management felt they were being treated fairly when they fought in Cleveland because Larry never seemed to have a problem lining up good fights and fighters to fill out his shows.

Larry was the matchmaker for over 19 years for Ed Bang's Cleveland News Toyshop Fund Shows held in December each year. Those shows featured four 10-round main events and raised money for toys to be given to underprivileged children.

The years 1940–1949 were without a doubt the most successful in professional boxing in Cleveland and were the boom years for the arena when it came to local promotions.

All fight shows from the second half of the 1940s appear here in order, with contenders and fight results.

January 16, 1945: Sugar Ray Robinson won a 10-round unanimous decision over Tommy Bell, Bobby Richardson won by a KO 2 over Johnny Eaton, and Leroy Jackson knocked out Ted Christie in the fourth round with a time of 2:18. The referee was Charlie Kivi. In other bouts, Bob Blevins won a six-round decision over Stanley Myka, and Ray Standifer lost a five-round unanimous decision to Johnny Clark.

February 27, 1945: Jimmy Bivins won a 10-round decision over Johnny Flynn, Freddie Schott won by a TKO in the fourth round over Bob Blevins, Johnny Lawer won by a KO 2 over Mario Raul Ochoa, Leroy Jackson knocked out Vito Mangine in the second round, Lee Garrett won a five-round decision over Joe Genovese, and Danny Freeman won a KO 3 over Gene Lydell.

March 7, 1945: Tommy Bell won by a KO 6 over Bobby Richardson. The time was 1:13 when referee Lou Parker counted Richardson out. On the undercard, Chuck Hunter won by a TKO 1 over Alex Doyle at only 0:49 due to referee Jackie Davis stopping the fight. Leroy Jackson knocked out Ted Christie in the second round, Lee Garrett won a five-round decision over Stanley Christie, and Berry Wright knocked out Lee Sheppard in the second round (the time was 1:56). Gene Lydell won a four-round decision over Tiger Brown in Brown's debut. The promoter was Bob Brickman.

March 21, 1945: Johnny Flynn won a 10-round decision over Lee Q. Murray. On the undercard, Harry Jeffra, former world bantamweight champion, won an eight-round decision over Cleveland's Leroy Jackson, Lee Garrett won a five-round decision over Johnny Virgo, and Joey Pirrone of Cleveland knocked out Patsy Zoccano in round one.

April 4, 1945: Chuck Hunter lost a 10-round split decision to Jimmy Doyle in the main event. On the undercard, former champion Harry Jeffra once against won an eight-round decision over Leroy Jackson, Artie Levine stopped Willie Watkins by a TKO in the fourth round, Lee Garrett lost a five-round decision to Johnny Virgo, and Eddie Martin won a five-round unanimous decision over Cleveland's Tony Brush in his ring debut.

May 9, 1945: Tommy Bell won by a TKO 5 over Chuck Hunter. On the undercard, Leroy Jackson won an eight-round decision over Victor Flores, Nava Esparza won by a KO 1 over Johnny Dawson, Lee Garrett won a six-round split decision over Johnny Virgo, Lloyd Gullick knocked out Gene Lydell in the second round, and Chuck Lloyd won by a KO 4 over Gordon Hunt. Gullick and Lloyd were making their ring debuts.

July 19, 1945: Tommy Bell lost by a 10-round unanimous decision to Jimmy Doyle. Scores were 6-4, 6-4, and 7-3. Vince Dell'Orto lost a six-round decision to Billy Eddy, Johnny Virgo won by a TKO 5 over Rudy Zadell with a time of 2:47. The referee was Benny Gershe. Burl Charity won a KO 2 over Tony DeCarlo, Juan Manuel lost a six-round unanimous decision to Chuck Lloyd, and Earl Mock knocked out Tom Walsh in the second round in what was Walsh's debut.

October 11, 1945: Chuck Hunter won a big victory with a 10-round unanimous decision over "California" Jackie Wilson. In other bouts, Mayon Padlo lost by a TKO 2 to Cleveland's Bobby Richardson, heavyweight Elmer Ray stopped Jimmy Gardner in the first round. The time was 0:46, and the referee was Joe Louis. Larry Ray won a six-round decision over Charley Weldon, and Marty Ferro won a four-rounder over Johnny Varcy.

October 29, 1945: "California" Jackie Wilson won by a TKO 5 over Frankie Terry. The time was 2:57. On the undercard, Rudy Zadell lost a six-round decision to Roy Lewis, Charley Padalino won a six-round split decision over Jack Hill, Tommy Rotolo won by a TKO 3 over Jim Carroll, Jerry Berthiaume won by a KO 2 over Charley Lomski, and Chuck Lloyd won a KO 1 over Chico Mars.

November 12, 1945: Chuck Hunter won a 10-round unanimous decision over Reuben Shank, scores were referee Jackie Davis, 4-6; judge Billy Sultzman, 3-7; and judge Herb Williams, 4-6. Jerry Berthiaume knocked out Ray Cobb at 0:37 of the opening round, Cleveland's Bobby Berry stopped Henry Jackson in the third round, Billy Walker stopped Art Robinson in the second round, Bobby Lalonde won by a KO 3 over Chuck Lloyd, and Pedro Juarez won a four-round decision over Danny Freeman.

December 3, 1945: At the annual Cleveland News Toyshop Fund Boxing Show, Jimmy Doyle stopped former world lightweight champion Lew Jenkins via a fourth-round TKO when referee Jackie Davis stopped the bout due to a bad cut under Jenkins's right eye. It had been a lopsided fight up until the stoppage. On the undercard, Tami Mauriello won by a KO 2 over Jerry Berthiaume. The time was 2:05, and the guest referee was Jack Dempsey. In other bouts, Leroy Jackson won an eight-round split decision over Lee Garrett, Billy Walker won a six-round decision over Augie Fleischauer, Bobby Lalonde won a six-round decision over Rudy Zadell, and Billy Miller won a six-round decision over Bobby Root. Attendance was 13,000 with a gate of $71,000.

January 14, 1946: Artie Levine knocked out Billy Walker in the ninth round; the time was 2:23. On the undercard, Leroy Jackson won an eight-round decision over Lee Garrett, Davey Feld knocked out Al King in the second round, Chuck Lloyd won a four-round decision over Ray Miller, and Howie Brodt stopped Pete McNamara in the first round.

February 25, 1946: Jimmy Bivins's undefeated streak of 27 came to an end when Jersey Joe Walcott won a 10-round split decision. The scoring was 6-4 for Bivins, 9-1 for Walcott, and 5-4-1 for Bivins. The judge with the last scorecard gave the fight to Walcott because he had knocked down Bivins for an eight count in round seven. On the undercard, Tommy Yarosz won a six-round decision over Charley Padalino, Gus Mullner lost by a KO 4 to Johnny Allen, Davey Feld won a six-round decision over Bobby Berry, Mike Birskovich (in his debut) lost a six-round decision to Otis Walker, and George Saunders knocked out Cleveland's Willie Muldune in round one. Attendance was 12,166 with a gate of $51,895.50.

March 11, 1946: Artie Levine stopped Jimmy Doyle by a TKO at 0:57 of the ninth round. Doyle suffered a severe head injury after building up a big lead in the fight after eight rounds. He was knocked down three times and ended up in the hospital; the injury threatened his career. In other bouts, Leroy Jackson won a six-round decision over Artie Price, Rudy Zadell knocked out Nello Nucelli in the third round, Bobby Root decisioned Clevelander Joey Kushner in a six-round bout, Al King knocked out Gib Jones in the first round, and Mike Birskovich knocked out Eddie Miller in the first round.

March 25, 1946: Pat Comiskey won by a fourth-round kayo over Al King, Sammy Secreet won a 10-round decision over Billy Walker, and Davey Feld won a 10-round decision over George Saunders. Feld scored three knockdowns in round six. In other bouts, Leroy Jackson won a 10-round decision over Lee Garrett; Arthur Brown won by a KO 2 over Bill Taylor, who was making his debut; Mike Birskovich won a four-round decision over Al Thornton; and Cleveland's Sammy Derrico won a four-round decision over Chet Bossio.

April 8, 1946: Sammy Secreet won a 10-round split decision over Harold Green. (Secreet had been in the US Navy from 1943 to 1946.) In the cofeature Tommy Yarosz won by a KO 3 over Wally Baden, Charley Padalino won by a third-round kayo over Rudy Turner, Billy Garrett won by a KO 1 over Bud Kelly, Pete McNamara stopped Tad DiLoreto in the second round, and Mike Birskovich stopped Billy Shaw in the second round.

April 20, 1946: Chester Rico won a 10-round decision over Lee Garrett. Garrett was down for a nine count in the first round. Phil Terranova, former NBA featherweight champion, knocked out Leroy Jackson in the sixth round. In other bouts, Charley Padalino won by a KO 8 over Billy Walker, Tommy Yarosz won by a TKO 4 over Jerry Berthiaume. The Cleveland Boxing Commission impounded Berthiaume's $1,000 purse for quitting after the third round with complaints of an injured hand because Xrays taken later showed nothing. In other bouts, Pete Spotti won by a TKO 3 over Pete McNamara, and Mike Birskovich won by a KO 2 over Billy Stemmier.

May 13, 1946: Harold Green got revenge over Sammy Secreet, winning a 10-round unanimous decision. In other bouts, Charley Padalino won by a KO 2 over Johnny Smith, Al Diaz won a six-round decision over Billy Stemmier, Eddie Perry won a six-round decision over John Chatmon, Paul Carbetta won by a TKO 4 over Buddy Smallwood, and Junius Woods won a four-round decision over Marty Ferro.

May 29, 1946: Artie Levine won by a TKO 3 over Charley Padalino. Referee Jackie Davis stopped the fight at 2:00. A.C. Rogers lost an eight-round decision to Mike Birskovich, Jimmy McDonough won by a TKO 6 over Al Diaz, who had suffered a badly cut left eye. Frankie Abrams won a six-round unanimous decision over Georgie Toy, and Luther Burgess stopped Joey Salcone, who was making his debut, in the opening round. Al Ellis won a four-round decision over Ross Sanchez, who was also making his ring debut.

June 10, 1946: Jimmy Bivins lost a 10-round unanimous decision to Lee Q. Murray. Steve Belloise, former New York State middleweight champion, stopped Billy Carrigan in the opening round. Buddy Garcia won by a KO 1 over Lee Garrett, Georgie Toy won by a KO 3 over Len Nelson, and Leroy Koeth won by a KO 1 over Partee Burk. Koeth was making his ring debut.

September 9, 1946: Sammy Secreet lost again to Harold Green, this time by 12-round split decision. Joey Ferrier lost an eight-round split decision to Al Highers, Lee Garrett won a six-round unanimous decision to Chucho Ruiz, Art Hardy lost by a KO 2 to Jimmy Mulligan with a time of 2:05. Jack McCurry lost by a TKO 3 to Jimmy Brown; the time was 0:58. Frankie Muche won a four-round decision over Leroy Koeth.

November 6, 1946: Sugar Ray Robinson stopped Artie Levine at 2:41 of the 10th round as referee Jackie Davis counted Levine out. Robinson was almost kayoed in the fourth round following a left hook and right cross by the hard-punching Levine. Robinson barely made it up and had several other close calls during the contest. The heavier Levine's punching was taking its toll on Robinson according to the January 1947 edition of *The Ring* magazine. Robinson switched his attack to the body and then the head in the 10th round and floored Levine. Attendance was 12,102, and Robinson received a purse of $12,500. In the other bouts, Charley Padalino won a 10-round decisen over Mike Birskovich, Lee Garrett won an eight-round decision over Oscar Wright, Joe Discepoli won a four-round decision over Leroy Koeth, Jerry Heminger won by a KO 1 over Sonny Jordan, and Larry Johnson in his ring debut stopped Al Marotti in round one.

December 3, 1946: At the annual Cleveland News Toyshop Fund Boxing Show, Carlos Chavez won a 10-round decision over Charley Cabey Lewis. On the undercard, Artie Levine stopped Jimmy Sheppard by a TKO 6; Charley Padalino lost a 10-round decision to Mike Birskovich; Bernard Docusen won by a TKO 7 over Joey Ferrier, who was floored seven times; and Frankie Muche won a five-round decision over Leroy Koeth. Attendance was 10,489 with a gate of $61,624.

February 24, 1947: Ralph Zannelli lost a 10-round split decision to Jimmy Doyle. Scores were 2-8, 5-4, and 3-7. In other bouts, Jimmy Hayden won by a TKO 9 over Danny Rosati due to a cut eye, Chuck Hunter won a 10-round decision over Jerry Fiorello, Jackie Lyons was knocked out in the third round by Bert Dowdell, and Bobby Burns won by a TKO 2 over Tommy Nichols.

March 10, 1947: Ezzard Charles knocked out Jimmy Bivins at 1:17 in the fourth round. It was Bivins's first knockout loss in Cleveland. Mike Birskovich lost by a TKO in the fifth round to Charley Hayes when referee Tony LaBranch stopped the contest at the 2:49 mark because of a badly cut left eyebrow. Lloyd Gibson won a five-round decision over Eddie Taylor, Larry Johnson won a five-round unanimous decision over Joe Discepoli, and Jackie Lyons won a RTD 3 over Lou Ogletree.

March 24, 1947: Jimmy Doyle won a 10-round decision over Danny Kapilow. According to the June 1947 edition of *The Ring* magazine, Doyle won at least six rounds. Omelio Agramonte won an eight-round decision over "Tiger" Ted Lowry, Billy Tierney won an eight-round decision over Larry Johnson, Charley Hayes won by a TKO 4 over Russell Baxter, Buddy Holderfield won a five-round decision over Johnny Rowe, and Joe Kezele won by a KO 3 over Henry Smith.

April 15, 1947: Chuck Hunter knocked out Larry Fontana in the fourth round. In the cofeature, Omelio Agramonte stopped Johnny Holloway in the opening round. In other bouts, Billy Tierney won by a TKO 8 over Larry Johnson; Mike Birskovich won by a TKO 2 over Bobby Burns; Matt Yannie, in his ring debut, won a four-round decision over Joe Kezele; and Bill Farmer won a four-round decision over Dick Mansfield.

May 12, 1947: Chuck Hunter stopped Artie Levine at 1:12 of the ninth round with referee Joe Sedley counting out Levine. Bob Amos won an eight-round decision over Davey Feld, Sammy Secreet won an eight-round decision over Bobby Richardson, Clem Fitzpatrick won an eight-round decision over Billy Tierney, Jimmy Sanders won a four-round decision over Bill Farmer, and Joe Discepoli stopped Willie Sivillo by a third-round TKO. Larry Atkins was the promoter.

June 24, 1947: Sugar Ray Robinson defended his world welterweight championship for the first time against Jimmy Doyle. The Irishman was giving a pretty good account of himself, and according to local write-ups, Doyle carried the sixth and seventh rounds. But in the eighth round, Robinson launched a flurry of punches, and Doyle's legs stiffened and he fell backwards his full length, hitting his head to the canvas with a resounding thud. He started to get up but at the count of seven fell back down. The bell rang as referee Jackie Davis reached the count of nine. Doyle's corner lifted him to his stool but immediately told Davis he could not continue, thus Robinson was awarded the fight by a TKO. When Doyle could not be revived after 15 minutes, he was rushed to St. Vincent Charity Hospital where he was found to have suffered a brain concussion and a hemorrhage. A brain specialist was called, and Doyle underwent surgery five hours after the fight. Doyle never regained consciousness and died 17 hours later. The other bouts saw Artie Towne stop Henry Brimm by a TKO in the eighth round, Mike Birskovich knocked out Clem Fitzpatrick in the second round, Jimmy Sanders won a five-round decision over Joey Ferrier, Julius Menendez won a five-round decision over Ernie Pelaia, and Otis Walker won a five-round decision over Larry Johnson. Attendance was 10,089.

November 12, 1947: Steve Belloise, former New York State middleweight champion, won by a TKO 2 over Mike Birskovich. In other bouts, Jimmy Edgar won by a KO 2 over Davey Feld, Pat Comiskey knocked out "Big Boy" Brown in the fifth round, and Tommy Bell won a 10-round split decision over Billy Cooper. Scores were 6-4, 3-7, and 5-4. Ritchie Shinn won by a TKO 4 over "Bulldog" Camaqueyano.

December 2, 1947: At the annual Cleveland News Toyshop Fund Boxing Show, Ezzard Charles stopped a bloody Fitzie Fitzpatrick in round four by a TKO. The time was 1:34 when referee Jackie Davis stopped the fight. On the undercard, Chuck Hunter lost a 10-round split decision to Jimmy Edgar, Steve Belloise knocked out Billy Arnold in the first round, Mickey Doyle won a 10-round split decision over Sonny Horne, Jackie Keough won a four-round unanimous decision over Joe Kezele, and Jimmy Varketta won a four-round unanimous decision over Lee Garrett. Attendance was 13,384 with a gate of $83,648.

January 13, 1948: Ezzard Charles knocked out Archie Moore at 2:40 of the eighth round; referee Jackie Davis counted Moore out. In other bouts, Chuck Hunter won a 10-round unanimous decision over Dave Clark, Mickey Doyle won a 10-round unanimous decision over Charley Padalino, Elkin Brothers won by a TKO 3 over Al Smith, Jackie Keough lost a five-round split decision to Jackie Armitage, and Lloyd Gibson knocked out Tony DeMicco in the opening round.

March 16, 1948: Steve Belloise won by a TKO 7 over Mickey Doyle; the time was 0:33. On the undercard, Chuck Hunter won a 10-round decision over Cecil Hudson, Lloyd Gibson won by a TKO 6 over Charley Hayes, Harold Dettman won a four-round decision over Johnny Komio, Danny Johnson won a four-round decision over Bob Calloway, and Luis Ramos knocked out Kuko Ortiz in the third round.

April 20, 1948: Pat Valentino lost a 10-round unanimous decision to Jimmy Bivins. Scores were 8-2, 5-4, and 6-4. Chuck Hunter won a 10-round split decision over Steve Belloise, Buddy Garcia won by a TKO 9 over Joey Carkido, Mickey Doyle won by a TKO 6 over Lou Valles, and Joey Salcome won a four-round unanimous decision over Juan Manuel.

November 17, 1948: Nick Barrone won a 10-round decision over Chuck Hunter. On the undercard, Harry LaSane won a 10-round decision over Cleveland's Eddie Marotta; Paulie Brooks, also from Cleveland, won a six-round decision over Harry Marshall; George Kolarik won a four-round decision to Allie Gronik; and Ricky Ronci won by a KO 2 over Paulie Simpson, who was making his debut. Also, Jimmy Bivins and Joe Louis fought a six-round exhibition at this show.

December 7, 1948: At the annual Cleveland News Toyshop Fund Boxing Show, Joey Maxim won a 10-round split decision over hometown rival Jimmy Bivins. Scores were 4-6, 5-4, and 5-4. Sandy Saddler knocked out Eddie Giosa in the second round; the time was 1:34. Reuben Jones won a 10-round unanimous decision over Anton Raadik, and Pete Mead won a 10-round decision over Mickey Doyle. In two other prelim bouts, Steve King won a five-round unanimous decision over Ricky Ronci, and Paulie Brooks won by a TKO 3 over Bobby Lalonde, time 1:54. Attendance was 12,500 with a gate of $65,602.

February 22, 1949: Chuck Hunter won a 10-round split decision over Artie Levine. In other bouts, Dick Wagner stopped Billy Fox by a TKO 9 at 0:48 of the round, Jean Walzack won a 10-round split decision over Jimmy Sanders, Reuben Jones won by a TKO 8 over Mickey Doyle, Pete McNamara won a five-round split decision over George Kolarik, and Ted Fittipaldo won a five-round unanimous decision over Johnny Gill.

March 10,1949: Dick Wagner made it two in a row over Billy Fox, knocking him out at 2:14 of the sixth round by a TKO when referee Jackie Davis stopped the fight. On the undercard, Vince Turpin won a 10-round decision over Chico Pacheco, Georgie Small won by a KO 10 over Kenny Barton, Dan Moray won a five-round split decision over Paulie Simpson, and Johnny Bernardo won by a KO 3 over Johnny Varcy. The time was 0:12.

March 21, 1949: Tommy Yarosz won a 10-round unanimous decision over Chuck Hunter. In other bouts, Vince Turpin won a 10-round unanimous decision over Jimmy Sherrer, George "Wildman" Henry won a 10-round decision over Tom McKeagney, Johnny Rowe won a five-round decision over Ronnie Hamlin, and Dan Moray won a four-round decision over Roland Streety.

March 28, 1949: Lee Sala won a 10-round unanimous decision over Georgie Small. Scores were 6-3, 5-4, and 6-4. On the undercard, George "Wildman" Henry won a 10-round split decision over Bee Wright, Jesse Underwood won a 10-round split decision over Anthony Arnone, Allie Gronik won a five-round decision over Joe Kezele, and Ted Fittipaldo won a five-round decision over Bill Foley.

April 11, 1949: Dick Wagner won a 10-round split decision over Artie Levine. Scores were 6-4, 7-3, and 4-5. Chuck Hunter won a 10-round unanimous decision over Chubby Wright, Dan Moray won a six-round decision over Johnny Bassett, Johnny Rowe won a five-round decision over Frankie Muche, and Jerry Fleming won by a TKO 5 over Harry Moore, who was making his ring debut.

April 22, 1949: Ike Williams won by a TKO at 2:21 of the sixth round over Vince Turpin. In other bouts, Allie Gronik won a 10-round decision over Johnny Bernardo, Georgie Small won a 10-round unanimous decision over Tony Riccio, Johnny Rowe won a six-round unanimous decision over Louis Joyce, and Frankie Muche won by a TKO 4 over Charlie Scott. The time was 2:48, and the referee was Lou Parker.

May 2, 1949: Robert Villemain won a 10-round unanimous decision over Reuben Jones, Jackie Keough of Cleveland won an eight-round decision over George Chape, Bob Golden won a six-round decision over Dan Moray, Allie Gronik won a six-round decision over Johnny Paoletti, and George Kolarik won a six-round decision over Ronnie Hamlin.

June 20, 1949: Jimmy Bivins, weighing 186 pounds, won a 10-round unanimous decision over Willie Bean, who weighed 204 pounds. Dick Wagner knocked out Artie Levine in the eighth round. The time was 0:18 when referee Jackie Davis counted Levine out. In other bouts, Paulie Brooks won by a third-round TKO over Paddy Hill, Freddie Jones won by a TKO 3 over Clay Milliron, and Johnny Izzo won by a TKO 6 over Jimmy Casson. The time for that bout was 1:48, and the referee was Benny Gershe.

October 25, 1949: Bobby Dykes won an eight-round decision over "California" Jackie Wilson; Chuck Hunter won by an eight-round decision over Alvin Williams; and Orlando Zulueta, Cuban welterweight, won an eight-round decision over Dave Marsh. In other bouts, Jackie Keough won an eight-round decision over Raul Perez, and Guillermo Gimenez won by eight-round decision over Buddy Garcia.

December 6, 1949: At the Cleveland News Toyshop Fund Boxing Show, Sandy Saddler won a 10-round split decision over Orlando Zulueta. Scores were referee Vito Mazzeo, 4-5; judge Charley Bill, 5-4; and judge John Sayanek, 5-4. The bout was listed for the vacant world junior lightweight title, recognized by the NBA. On the undercard, Rocky Graziano, former middleweight champion, won a 10-round majority decision over Sonny Horne. Scores were 8-2, 5-5, and 7-3. In other bouts, Chuck Hunter won a 10-round decision over Dick Wagner, Eddie Marotta won a 10-round unanimous decision over Lino Garcia, and Lalu Sabotin won by a TKO 3 over Tony Leo Pietras; the time was 2:29. It was announced that this was the largest indoor crowd in Cleveland's history at the time, with 14,202 in attendance.

Pictured here is a section of the Republic Steel Corporation in 1946. Cleveland was a blue-collar town in those days and that helped produce some excellent, tough fighters and fight fans. The city had two very large companies in Republic Steel and Jones and Laughlin (J&L) Steel as well as a smaller US Steel plant. The author actually worked for Republic Steel, which later became LTV Steel, for 30 years. (Courtesy of Michael Schwartz Library, Cleveland State University.)

Jackie Keough was a native Clevelander who had great success in the amateurs, winning local Golden Gloves, National Golden Gloves, and National AAU championships at 147 pounds in 1947. As a professional, Keough fought some of the best welterweights and middleweights—Gene Hairston, Bobby Dykes, and Randolph Turpin—but only fought on three arena cards in the 1940s and 1950s.

Sugar Ray Robinson was, pound for pound, one of the greatest fighters ever. The world welterweight and five-time middleweight champion fought four times at the arena from 1942 to 1947.

Harry Jeffra, former world bantamweight and featherweight champion, met Cleveland's Leroy Jackson twice in 1945 and won two eight-round decisions. Jeffra's career spanned from 1933 to 1950, and he fought in 128 bouts.

Jimmy Bivins jabs at Jersey Joe Walcott, future heavyweight champion, on February 25, 1946. This arena show was Walcott's only appearance in Cleveland, and he won a controversial 10-round split decision. The fight, which derailed Bivins in his quest for a heavyweight title bid while ending a 27-win streak, launched Walcott into contention.

Jimmy Doyle (left) and Artie Levine (right) exchange punches on March 11, 1946. Levine won the contest at 0:57 of the ninth round by a technical knockout. (Photograph by Norbert J. Yassanye, *Plain Dealer*.)

Harold Green, a Brooklyn, New York, middleweight contender, fought from 1942 to 1953. Green had career wins over Ernie Durando and twice defeated Rocky Graziano. He also stopped future middleweight champion Joey Giardello in 1950. At the arena, Green fought three times in 1946, winning two out of three 10-round decisions against Sammy Secreet, and he fought once in 1950, winning a 10-round decision over Ernie Durando.

AT HOME
BOXING
FEB. 24
ARENA
DOYLE
HUNTER
ZANELLI
FIORELLO
BOND CLO

At the Cleveland Arena on February 24, 1947, the crowd lines up to see Jimmy Doyle versus Ralph Zanelli. (Courtesy of Michael Schwartz Library, Cleveland State University.)

Referee Joe Sedley counts out Artie Levine in the ninth round on May 12, 1947, as Cleveland's Chuck Hunter scored the knockout victory.

Jimmy Doyle and champion Sugar Ray Robinson greet each other prior to their June 24, 1947, world welterweight title bout, which ended in tragedy. Robinson stopped Doyle in the eighth round, and he never regained consciousness, dying in a local hospital after surgery the next day.

Sugar Ray Robinson floors challenger Jimmy Doyle in the fateful eighth round on June 24, 1947. Doyle was seriously hurt and died 17 hours later after having surgery. The fight, stopped in the eighth round, was a competitive contest up until that time. This was Robinson's first defense of his welterweight title.

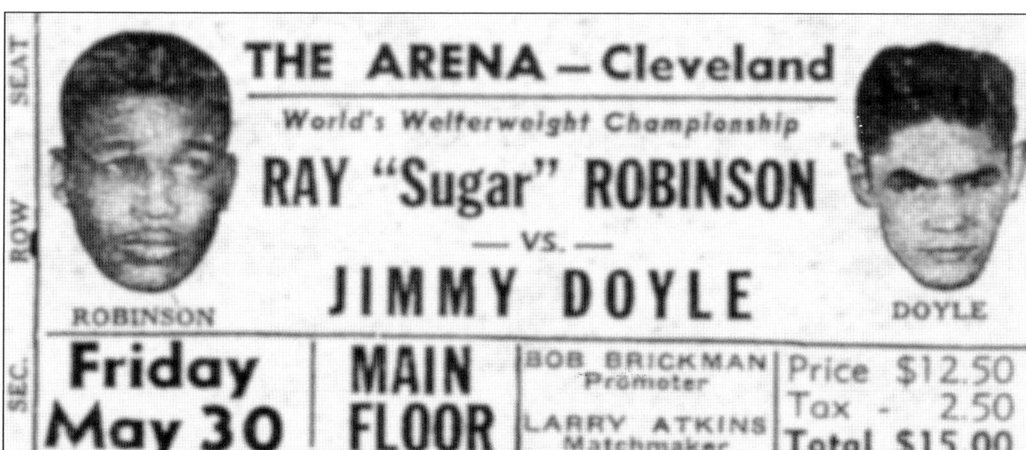

Pictured above is the fight ticket from the June 24, 1947, Robinson–Doyle welterweight title fight. Doyle was knocked out in the eighth round and seriously hurt. He died 17 hours later.

Billy Arnold, a middleweight contender in the 1940s, in his only appearance at the Cleveland Arena, was knocked out in the opening round by former top contender Mike Belloise at the December 2, 1947, Cleveland News Toyshop Fund Boxing Show.

Pictured is the crowd of fight fans at the 1947 Cleveland News Toyshop Fund Boxing Show at the arena.

Ezzard Charles was one of the best fighters to ever come out of Ohio. As a light-heavyweight, he dominated several excellent fighters such as Jimmy Bivins, Lloyd Marshall, Archie Moore, and Joey Maxim. He would go on to win the vacated heavyweight title against Jersey Joe Walcott in 1949. Charles fought at the arena four times in the 1940s.

Hilton "Fitzie" Fitzpatrick lies battered on the canvas as Ezzard Charles strides away. Charles won by a fourth-round KO at the December 2, 1947, Cleveland News Toyshop Fund Boxing Show. This was the second time Charles had beaten Fitzpatrick in 1947.

Archie Moore was one of the best light-heavyweight champs ever. His only Cleveland Arena appearance resulted in his eighth-round kayo defeat against Ezzard Charles, the "Cincinnati Cobra," on January 13, 1948.

On January 13, 1948, future world heavyweight champion Ezzard Charles of Cincinnati, Ohio, knocks out future world light-heavyweight champion Archie Moore in the eighth round to make it three in a row over Moore.

Pat Valentino was a West Coast heavyweight contender in the 1940s. On April 20, 1948, he lost a 10-round unanimous decision to Jimmy Bivins.

Winners at the 1948 Cleveland News Toyshop Fund Boxing Show were Joey Maxim, Sandy Saddler, Ruben Jones, and Pete Mead. Attendance was 12,500 with a gate of $65,602.

Anton Raadik, an Estonian middleweight based out of Chicago, fought at the December 7, 1948, Cleveland News Toyshop Fund Boxing Show, losing a 10-round unanimous decision to Reuben Jones.

Chuck Hunter came out of the amateur ranks of the Cleveland Golden Gloves as the 1943 national champion at 135 pounds, and became a world-ranked welterweight in the pro ranks. From 1943 to 1953, he had 72 bouts, with 28 of them being at the Cleveland Arena, more than any other fighter. He was a crowd favorite.

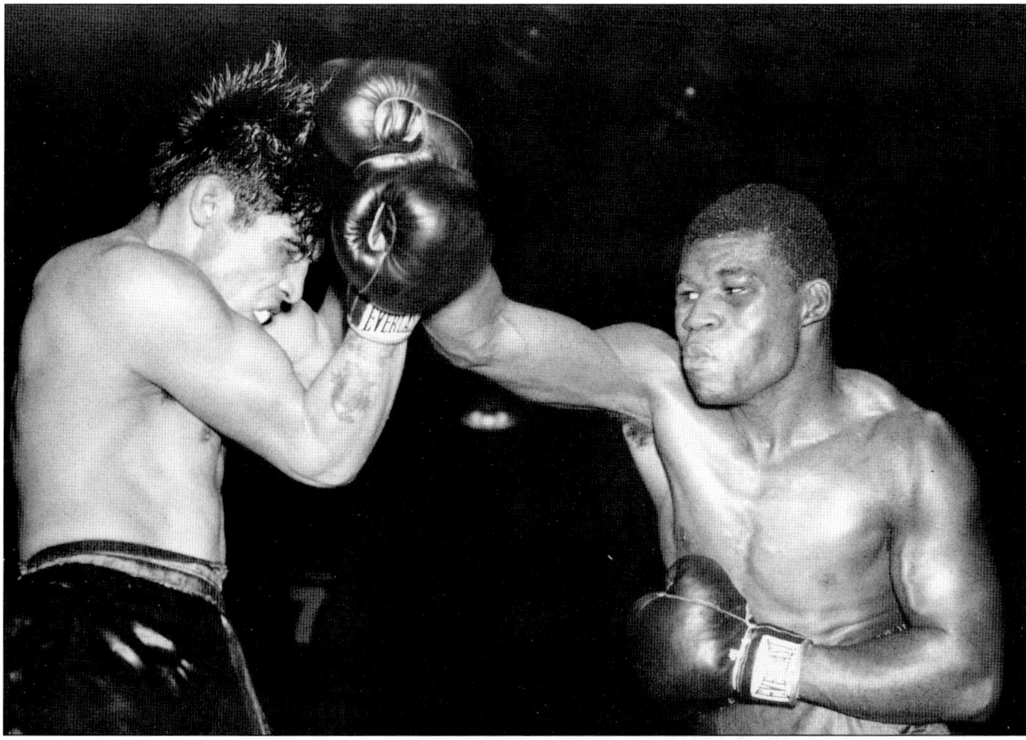

Welterweight Chuck Hunter lands a right hand on Alvin Williams as he pounded out an eight-round decision on October 25, 1949. (Photograph by Bill Nehez.)

Chuck Hunter holds off the charging Dick Wagner on December 6, 1949, one of several Cleveland News Toyshop Fund Boxing Shows he fought in. Hunter won a 10-round decision.

Rocky Graziano, former middleweight champion, fought only once at the arena—at the December 6, 1949, Cleveland News Toyshop Fund Boxing Show, winning a majority 10-round decision over Sonny Horne of Niles, Ohio.

Sandy Saddler is showing off his new championship belt he received for winning the vacant world junior lightweight title over Orlando Zulueta of Cuba by 10-round decision on December 6, 1949, at the annual Cleveland News Toyshop Fund Boxing Show. (Photograph by Bob Runyan.)

Tommy Yarosz was a Pittsburgh light-heavyweight who was very popular in Cleveland and fought at the arena six times in the 1940s.

Joey Maxim, the pride of Collinwood, not only won the local Cleveland Golden Gloves but also was the National Golden Gloves champion at 160 pounds and the National AAU champion at the same weight in 1940. As a professional from 1941 to 1958, he was the world light-heavyweight champion from 1950 to 1952. He had career wins over Jimmy Bivins, Freddie Mills (to win the title), Jersey Joe Walcott, Gus Lesnevich, Sugar Ray Robinson, and Floyd Patterson.

Jackie Wilson, a local product, was amazing as an amateur, winning the local Cleveland Golden Gloves, National Golden Gloves, and AAU in 1936 at 112 pounds. His only loss was at the 1936 Olympics to Ulderico Sergo of Italy by a close decision, thus winning the silver medal and finishing 50-1. As a pro, he was world ranked as a welterweight. He had 88 fights, most of them in California, but he did fight five times at the arena in the 1940s. He is seen here at a local gym posing with a poster promoting his upcoming bout with Sammy Secreet at the Cleveland Arena.

Four

THE 1950s

The 1940s were a hard act to follow. Although some very good fights were still being held at the arena in the 1950s, including Ed Bang's Cleveland News Toyshop Fund Boxing Shows held in December, fight cards were scheduled much less often. For example, 1950 only had four shows and 1951 only one. The year 1953 was the only one during the decade with more than six shows. Where 80 shows had been held in the 1940s, only 37 were held in the 1950s.

There were many theories as to why the fight business in Cleveland and other cities had slowed down. One was the oversaturation of televised boxing. The television was becoming a normal thing in many households, and one did not have to leave the couch to witness some very good fight action.

One thing that remained consistent was the fact that Larry Atkins was still able to match up quality fighters when he could schedule cards at the arena. Among those appearing were champions, soon to be champions, or former champions such as Jake LaMotta, Sandy Saddler, Kid Gavilan, Joe Brown, Johnny Bratton, Ezzard Charles, Gene Fullmer, Joey Giardello, Carmen Basilio, Flash Elorde, and Sonny Liston.

Indeed, despite less than half the fight cards of the 1940s, arena fight shows in the 1950s still packed quite a punch.

All arena fight cards, fighters, and results of the 1950s are listed here in order.

March 28, 1950: Jake LaMotta won by a TKO in the sixth round over Cleveland's Chuck Hunter. Referee Jackie Davis stopped the fight at the 0:59 mark after Hunter had been down. On the undercard, Bob Flanagan lost by a TKO 2 to Dolph Quijano. The time was 2:38. Jimmy Sanders won a 10-round unanimous decision over Aldo Minelli, Paulie Simpson won a five-round decision over Virgil Strauss, and Charles Lester won by a KO 1 over Billy Sherman. Attendance was 8,181.

April 18, 1950: Sandy Saddler won by a TKO in the ninth round over Lauro Salas in defense of his world junior lightweight title. The time was 2:51 when referee Jackie Davis stopped the contest. In other bouts, Gino Buonvino won by a TKO 2 over Dolph Quijano, Billy Graham won a 10-round unanimous decision over Jimmy Sanders, Larry Shaw won a 10-round decision over Bob Flanagan, and Charles Lester won by a KO 1 over Tommy Woodward. The time was 0:58. Attendance was 6,000.

November 9, 1950: Ernie Durando won by a KO in fifth round over Joey DeJohn. The time was 2:10. On the undercard, Akron's Ronnie Delaney won a 10-round decision over Charley Cotton, Walter Cartier won by a TKO 4 over Joe Taylor; time was 2:10. Taylor had been knocked down three times. In other bouts, Allie Gronik won by a TKO 1 over Johnny Paoletti. (The bout was halted at 0:40 because of a badly cut eye). Kevin Allen, in his ring debut, knocked out Bobby Graham in the second round.

December 4, 1950: The Cleveland News Toyshop Fund Boxing Show featured Kid Gavilan, future welterweight champion, winning a 10-round unanimous decision over Youngstown's Tony Janiro. In other bouts, Harold Green won a 10-round split decision over Ernie Durando; Bob Baker won a 10-round unanimous decision over Abel Cestac; Walter Cartier won by a KO 8 over Jimmy Sherrer; and in a battle of Clevelanders, Tommy Salem won a four-round split decision over Mickey Mars. Attendance was 9,342 with a gate of $61,269.

December 5, 1951: In the only arena fight card of 1951, the Cleveland News Toyshop Fund Boxing Show featured Harry "Kid" Matthews winning by a 10-round unanimous decision over Danny Nardico. Scoring was referee Jackie Davis, 8-2; judge Charley Bill, 7-2; and judge Herb Williams, 7-2. In other bouts, Gene Hairston won by a TKO 5 over Charley Zivic. The time was 1:59 when referee Lou Parker stopped the contest. Chico Vejar won by a TKO in the fifth round over Terry Young. The time was 2:50, and the referee was Vito Mazzeo. Johnny Greco won by a KO 3 over Nick Mistovich. The time was 1:49, and the bout was refereed by Joe Sedley. Bobby Jackson, in his ring debut, won a four-round unanimous decision over Sonny Wilcox, also making his ring debut, and Tommy Salem won by a KO 1 over Bucky Gardner. The time was 0:50 before a house of 13,808.

March 19, 1952: Danny Nardico won a 10-round unanimous decision over Dick Wagner, who was down twice. The scoring was as follows: referee Jackie Davis, 6-4; judge Charley Bill, 5-3; and judge Herb Williams, 5-4. On the undercard, Ronnie Delaney won by s KO 10 over Eddie Smith, Elmer Lakatos won by a KO 3 over Al Gualteri, Chuck Higgins won a four-round decision over Bobby Jackson, Joey Greenwood won a four-round decision over Lou Quinn, and Lalu Sabotin won by a TKO 4 over Billy Hatcher.

April 18, 1952: Chico Vejar won a 10-round unanimous decision over Johnny "Red" DeFazio. Scoring was referee Jackie Davis, 6-4; judge Charley Bill, 7-3; and John Sayanek, 7-3. In other bouts, Danny Nardico won a 10-round unanimous decision over Lalu Sabotin, Jackie Keough won a 10-round unanimous decision over Richie Anderson, Elmer Lakatos won a TKO 2 over Paul Scott. The time for that bout was 2:12, and it was refereed by Vito Mazzeo. In the final bout, Howard Tate won a KO 2 over Ralph Heard.

September 3, 1952: Del Flanagan won a 10-round unanimous decision over Johnny "Red" DeFazio. On the undercard, Russ Jeffries won a TKO 8 over Joey Carkido, and Willie Troy won by a TKO 4 over Willie Wright. The time 1:48, and the bout was refereed by Lou Parker. Other bouts saw Rocky Casillo win by a TKO 3 over Wendell Delorme (time 1:40, referee Lou Parker), and Ral Prado won a KO 1 over Lou Quinn. The time was 1:10.

November 5, 1952: Dick Wagner won a 10-round unanimous decision over Lalu Sabotin. The scoring was as follows: referee Jackie Davis, 7-3; judge Charley Bill, 6-4; and judge John Sayanek, 8-2. On the undercard, Ronnie Delaney won an eight-round unanimous decision over Herbie Hayes, Pedro Gonzalez won an eight-round unanimous decision over Russ Jeffries, and Alan Moody won by a KO 1 over Rudy Flowers, who was making his debut. The time was 1:47, and the referee was Vito Mazzeo. Tony Anthony, in his debut, won an RFD 2 over George Boddie, also making his debut, and Jesse Rodriquez won a four-round unanimous decision over Al Bergevin.

December 10, 1952: At the Cleveland News Toyshop Fund Boxing Show, Joe Brown, future world lightweight champion, stopped Don Bowman in the first round. The time was 2:30, and the guest referee was Rocky Marciano. On the undercard, Rocky Castellani won a 10-round unanimous decision over Jimmy Flood, and Chuck Davey won by a TKO 3 over Fritzie Pruden. The time of the round was 2:32 when referee Jackie Davis stopped the contest. Ronnie Delaney won a 10-round unanimous decision over Herbie Hayes, Del Flanagan won a 10-round unanimous decision over Richie Anderson, Al Andrews won by a TKO 4 over Davey Miles, and Billy Gordon won a four-round unanimous decision over Mickey Branch. Attendance was 11,921.

January 7, 1953: Lester Felton won by a TKO in the fourth round when Del Flanagan suffered a bruised right elbow and could not continue. Jimmy Flood won by a RTD in the third round over Billy Tisdale, who could not come out for the fourth round. Joe Brown won an eight-round unanimous decision over Joey Greenwood. In other bouts, Ken Hobner lost by a TKO 7 to Elmer Lakatos (time 1:26, referee Don Gonzalez). Alan Moody won by a TKO 3 over Buddy Laine, and Eddie Crawford won by a TKO 1 against Russ Hubbard, who suffered a badly cut eye.

March 25, 1953: George Araujo won a 10-round unanimous decision over Teddy Davis. The scoring was referee Tony LaBranch, 7-2; judge Charley Bill, 7-3; and judge Herb Williams, 8-2. On the undercard, Ben Skelton knocked out Chuck Hunter at 2:57 of the first round; Doug Medley won an eight-round unanimous decision over Abdelkader Ben Miloud; Frank Favaro won by a KO 1 over Willie Reeves; Mickey Mars won by a TKO 2 over Russ Hubbard; and Willie Wilkerson won a four-round unanimous decision over Sal Brunello, who was making his debut.

April 14, 1953: Kid Gavilan, world welterweight champion, won a 10-round split decision over Livio Minelli. The scoring was as follows: referee Jackie Davis, 6-4; judge Charley Bill, 4-6; and Herb Williams, 5-4. In other bouts, Chico Vejar won a 10-round unanimous decision over Tony Cimmino, Chuck Hunter won an eight-round decision over Ben Skelton, Stonewall Jackson won an eight-round decision over Chuck Price, Billy Wagner knocked out Mickey Mars by a TKO in fourth round, and Bob Finnerty and Harry Miller ended up in a third-round no contest. The attendance was 10,151 with a gate of $53,602.

May 7, 1953: Johnny Bratton, former welterweight champion, won a 10-round unanimous decision over Livio Minelli. Scoring was referee Tony LaBranch, 5-3; judge John Sayanek, 7-2; and judge Herb Williams, 6-2. On the undercard, Abdelkader Ben Miloud won an eight-round unanimous decision over Doug Medley, and Chuck Hunter made it two in a row with an eight-round unanimous decision over Ben Skelton. In other bouts, crowd favorite Rocky Castellani won by a KO 1 over Johnny Mack; the time was 0:26. Andy Bohner won by a TKO 2 over Dick McKinney (time 1:08), and Mickey Mars won by a KO 6 over Billy Wagner (time 2:44).

June 17, 1953: Pierre Langlois lost a 10-round split decision to Rocky Castellani. Scoring was referee Jackie Davis, 4-6; judge Charley Bill, 3-6; and judge Herb Williams, 5-4. In other bouts, Alan Moody won by a TKO 2 over Eddie Bell, Sonny Bunn won by a KO 1 over William Brown, Bobby Finnerty knocked out John Lundell in the opening round, Charley Tilden won by a TKO 1 over Johnny Stit, and Mickey Mars won by a KO 4 over Jerry Kortright.

October 28, 1953: Rocky Castellani won a 10-round unanimous decision over Mickey Laurent, and Joey Giambra won by a TKO 1 over Don Oates. Referee Vito Mazzeo stopped the contest after Oates had been down twice. In other bouts, Henry Bronko won by eight-round unanimous decision over Al Costantino, Mickey Mars won by an eight-round unanimous decision over Herky Kaminsky, Bobby Jackson won a four-round split decision over Jimmy Glover, and Ted Tangles won a four-round decision over Frankie Masters; both men were making their pro debuts.

December 9, 1953: The Cleveland News Toyshop Fund Boxing Show featured Rocky Castellani continuing his winning ways in Cleveland with a 10-round unanimous decision over Gil Turner. The scoring was as follows: referee Lou Parker, 5-4; judge Charley Bill, 5-4; and judge Herb Williams, 6-3. Willie Troy won by a TKO 4 over Tuzo Portuguez, and Charley Norkus won by a TKO 2 over Hal Boylston. The referee was Vito Mazzeo. In other bouts, Mickey Mars, Cleveland Golden Gloves champion and national amateur bantamweight champion in 1949, won an eight-round unanimous decision over Herky Kaminsky in a featherweight bout. Other bouts saw Bobby Jackson winning a four-round split decision over Sonny Bunn, Eddie O'Hara losing a four-round decision to Clarence Butler, and Pete Edington (debut) winning by a KO 2 over Dick Holling. Attendance was listed as 11,813.

April 15, 1954: Rocky Castellani won a 10-round unanimous decision over Pedro Gonzales. In other bouts, former Olympic champion Nate Brooks lost a 10-round unanimous decision to Mickey Mars. Nate's brother Paulie Brooks won a 10-round decision over Jackie Blair, Jesse Rodriquez won a four-round decision over Nick Harris, Ted Tangles won a four-round decision over Cal Nathan, and Dan Moray won a four-round decision over Ike Bell.

December 1, 1954: The annual Cleveland News Toyshop Fund Boxing Show featured a very exciting heavyweight battle between Charlie Norkus and Roland LaStarza, with Norkus winning a 10-round unanimous decision. The scoring was as follows: referee Jackie Davis, 96-94; judge John Sayanek, 96-94; and judge George Sherman, 94-93. On the undercard, Rocky Castellani won by a TKO 8 over Moses Ward. The time was 2:30. Ward was down twice in the first round and twice in eighth. Tony Baldoni won an eight-round split decision over George Wallace, Frank Lentine won a six-round unanimous decision over Mickey Warner, and Mike DeJohn won by a KO 2 over Mack Cox (time 0:47). Tommy Elder, who was making his debut, won a four-round decision over Russ Hubbard. The attendance was 9,112 with a gate of $55,992.

January 12, 1955: Rocky Castellani won a 12-round unanimous decision over Holly Mims. The scores were lopsided in favor of Castellani: referee Tony LaBranch, 118-112; judge Charley Bill, 115-111; and judge Herb Williams, 116-109. In other bouts, Mike DeJohn won a six-round unanimous decision over Jimmy L. Williams, Tony Baldoni won by a TKO 2 over Ronnie Hamlin, Bobby Lee won a six-round decision over Ike Stevenson, Tommy Salem won a six-round decision over Ralph Cervantes, Guido Picone won a six-round split decision over Dick Brewer, Reybon Stubbs won a four-round decision over Young Kid Satan, and Bobby Jackson won by a TKO 3 over Emory Kirk in a fight between Cleveland middleweight boxers. The time was 1:56, and the bout was refereed by Don Gonzales.

August 31, 1955: Tommy Jackson won a 10-round unanimous decision over Ezzard Charles. The scoring was as follows: referee Lou Parker, 96-94; judge George Sherman, 97-88; and judge Herb Williams, 98-85. On the undercard, Jimmy Bivins won an RFD 3 when Dan Moray was unable to continue due to a damaged hand. In other fights, Gene Johns won an eight-round split decision over Hector Peralta, Mike DeJohn won a TKO 3 over Cleveland's Gene Jackson, Frank Williams won a four-round unanimous decision over Jimmy McMillian, and Mickey Savage won a four-round decision over Ernie Smith.

September 23, 1955: Ralph "Tiger" Jones won a 10-round unanimous decision over Chris Christensen, Ludwig Lightburn won an eight-round split decision over L.C. Morgan, Tommy Salem won a four-round decision over Benny Artist, Bobby Jackson won a four-round decision over Wilf Greaves, and Curtis Coles won by a KO 2 over Charles Harris.

October 28, 1955: Jimmy Slade won a 10-round split decision over Tommy "Hurricane" Jackson. Scoring was 98-94, 96-95, and 95-96. Rocky Castellani won by a TKO 10 over Pedro Gonzalez; Jimmy Bivins, in his last bout of a long career, won a six-round decision over Mike DeJohn; Tex Gonzalez won a six-round split decision over Gaspar Ortega; Said Khelfa won a six-round decision over Bobby Jackson; and Tommy Salem won a six-round split decision over Eli Leggett.

December 7, 1955: At the Cleveland News Toyshop Fund Boxing Show, Bob Baker of Pittsburgh won the heavyweight main event over Nino Valdes of Cuba by a 10-round unanimous decision. The scoring was as follows: referee Tony LaBranch, 97-95; judge Charley Bill, 98-92; judge Herb Williams, 99-91. In the other bouts, Eduardo Lausse won by a TKO 5 over Johnny Sullivan; Orlando Zulueta, a Cuban lightweight, won an eight-round unanimous decision over Walter Brown; Gaspar "Indian" Ortega won a six-round unanimous decision over Tex Gonzalez; Ernie Fann won a four-round decision over Gene Jackson of Cleveland; Calvin Butler won a four-round split decision over Bob Santos; and Sonny Madeiros won a four-round decision over Frank Collica. The attendance was 8,380 with a gate of $63,392.

January 4, 1956: Gene Fullmer, future world middleweight champion, ended Rocky Castellani's unbeaten Cleveland streak, winning a 10-round split decision by scores of 97-94, referee Lou Palmer; 92-95, judge Charley Bill; and 96-92, judge Herb Williams. Johnny Sullivan won an eight-round decision over Jackie King; Calvin Butler, a Cleveland heavyweight, won a six-round decision over Jack Nelson; Reybon Stubbs lost a six-round decision to Rudy Gwin; and Wilf Greaves won by a KO 3 over Clevelander Clint Martin.

March 28, 1956: L.C. Morgan won a 10-round unanimous decision over Ludwig Lightburn, who was knocked down in the first round; Morgan was down in the ninth. Scoring was 94-93, 94-93, and 97-88. On the undercard, Henry Hank won by a TKO 4 over Rudy Gwin; Cleveland lightweight Tommy Salem won a six-round decision over Tommy Elder; Jackie King won a six-round split decision over Joe Leudanski; Cleveland lightweight Solomon Boysaw (debut) won by a TKO 4 over Willie Epps; Tony Hughes, Cleveland heavyweight, won his debut by kayo in the third round on Mack Cox; Larry Wagner, Cleveland middleweight, won his debut by a TKO 3 over Frank Collica.

September 28, 1956: Joey Giardello, future middleweight champion and a Cleveland crowd favorite, knocked out Bobby Boyd in the fifth round. The time was 2:25. Boyd had been down twice in the fifth. On the undercard, Cleveland heavyweight Tony Hughes won by a TKO 1 over Len Richards. The fight was stopped by referee Vito Mazzeo at 1:45 of the round. Calvin Butler, another Cleveland heavyweight, won by a TKO 1 over George Kartalian, who suffered a badly cut eye. In other bouts, Solomon Boysaw won a six-round decision over Henry Hickman; Cecil Shorts, a Cleveland welterweight making his debut, won a four-round unanimous decision over

Wayman Dawson; Clarence Alford, a Cleveland middleweight, won a four-round decision over Henry McCullough; Larry Wagner, another Cleveland middleweight, won a four-round decision over Dick Cagney; and Ed Zaremba won by a KO 2 over Hank Lassure.

October 12, 1956: Rory Calhoun won by a TKO 8 over Johnny Sullivan. On the undercard, Tony Hughes won a KO 2 over Jim O'Connell, Calvin Butler lost a six-round decision to Johnny Harper, Solomon Boysaw won a KO 1 over Tony Grasso, Chuck Taylor won a six-round decision over Dudley Chavis, and Rudy Williams won a four-round decision over Gene Jackson.

December 14, 1956: The Cleveland News Toyshop Fund Boxing Show featured Yama Bahama winning a 10-round unanimous decision over Jimmy Martinez. Scores were 48-42, 48-42, and 46-45. The cofeature of the show saw Joey Giardello winning a 10-round unanimous decision over Charley Cotton. The scoring was as follows: referee Tony LaBranch, 50-42; judge Charley Bill, 49-41; and judge Herb Williams, 50-42. In other bouts, Solomon Boysaw won a six-round unanimous decision over Benny Artist, Nicki Gadson won a six-round unanimous decision over Alan Kennedy, Tony Hughes won by a KO 1 over Tony Leo Pietras, Clarence Alford won by a TKO 3 over Clint Martin, Cecil Shorts won by four-round unanimous decision over Willie Epps, and Larry Wagner won by a TKO 4 over Dick Cagney. The attendance was 9,031 with a gate of $61,752.

February 22, 1957: Carmen Basilio defended his world welterweight championship against former champion Johnny Saxton and won by a TKO 2. Saxton was knocked down in the second round by a left hook and was unsteady, and referee Tony LaBranch stopped the contest at 2:42 of the round. On the undercard, Solomon Boysaw, a Cleveland lightweight, won a six-round unanimous decision over Nicki Gadson, Gene Buzzello won by a TKO 2 over Alan Kennedy, and Cleveland heavyweight Tony Hughes won a five-round decision over Bob O'Brien. The referee was Joe Sedley. Cleveland welterweight Cecil Shorts won by a KO 2 over Tommy Rogers, who was making his ring debut. The referee was Mike Minnich. Clarence Alford, a Cleveland middleweight, won a four-round unanimous decision over Lee Owens, and Prince Johnson won by a KO 2 over Bob Ritter. The attendance was 8,514.

May 17, 1957: Joey Giardello won a 10-round split decision over Rory Calhoun. The scores were as follows: referee Lou Parker, 45-46; judge Charley Bill, 46-45; and judge Herb Williams, 47-45. On the undercard, Ernest Burford won a six-round decision over Pat Lowry, Tony Hughes won a six-round decision over Bob Biehler, Solomon Boysaw won a KO 3 over Herman Hinton, Rudy Williams won a KO 3 over Clarence Alford, and Clint Martin won a four-round decision over Ted Milhouse.

September 27, 1957: Joey Giardello won by a TKO in the seventh round over Bobby Lane. The referee was Tony LaBranch. In other bouts, Cecil Shorts won a six-round decision over Kid Chocolate, Johnny Gillespie won by a TKO 2 over Joe Gray, Ernest Burford won by a KO 3 over Billy Gillespie, Jackie Lennon won by a four-round decision over Dick White, Cleveland heavyweight Gene Jackson stopped Ted Davis in the first round, and Clint Martin won by a TKO 2 over Clarence Alford.

December 6, 1957: At the annual Cleveland News Toyshop Fund Boxing Show, Cuban welterweight Isaac Logart won a 12-round unanimous decision over Gaspar Ortega. The scores were as follows: referee Mike Minnich, 56-50; judge Bill Thompson, 55-52; and judge Herb Williams, 56-54. This bout was listed as a world welterweight title eliminator. On the undercard, Cecil Shorts won a unanimous 10-round decision over Larry Boardman, Solomon Boysaw won an eight-round split decision over Lulu Perez, Ernest Burford won an eight-round split decision over Wilf Greaves, and Tony Hughes won an eight-round unanimous decision over Bob O'Brien. The attendance was 6,314 with a gate of $34,990.

December 15, 1958: The only show of 1958 was the Cleveland News Toyshop Fund Boxing Show. In the feature, Rory Calhoun won a 10-round unanimous decision over Ralph Jones. The scoring was as follows: referee Mike Minnich, 47-43; judge Charley Bill, 45-44; and judge Herb Williams, 48-45. In other bouts, Solomon Boysaw defeated Jay Fullmer by an eight-round unanimous decision, and then heavyweight LaMar Clark ran his record to 27-0 when he knocked out Cornell Butler at 1:21 of the opening round. In what was supposed to be a four-man heavyweight eliminator event with Clark meeting three opponents, he knocked out his second opponent Allan Hedge at 0:35 of the first round, remaining undefeated at 28-0. However, he sprained his right hand in the second bout, so the third bout was cancelled. In other bouts, Alonzo Johnson won by a KO 4 over Rudy Williams, Don Fullmer won a six-round unanimous decision over Roscoe Shamblin, Cecil Shorts won a six-round unanimous decision over Herb Nichols, and Frank Trusso won a four-round unanimous decision over Tommy O'Connor. Attendance was 6,415 with a gate of $28,670.

July 29, 1959: Cleveland lightweight Solomon Boysaw won a 10-round unanimous decision over future junior lightweight champion Flash Elorde of the Philippines. The scores were as follows: referee Lou Parker, 48-43; Charles Vaughn, 48-43; and Herb Williams, 48-43. In a heavyweight fight, Robert Morrie McNeil won by a TKO 3 over Paulie Simpson, who was unable to continue because of an injured hand. In other bouts, Antonio Marcilla won a six-round decision over Smiley Jack Packer; Eli Leggett won a four-round unanimous decision over Jerry Wells, who was making his debut; and Gene Jackson knocked out Kenny Griggs in the third round.

November 4, 1959: Joey Giardello won a 10-round unanimous decision over Dick Tiger. Scores were as follows: referee Don Gonzales, 45-44; judge Charley Bill, 45-44; and judge Herb Williams, 47-45. Roscoe Shamblin won a six-round decision over Clarence Alford, Gene Jackson won a six-round decision over Art Miller, Tony Hughes won a six-round decision over Chubby Duez, Antonio Marcilla won by a TKO 6 over Guido Picone, Joe Bertone won by a KO 1 over Tommy Weaver (debut), and Richie Craft won a four-round decision over Jerry Wells.

December 9, 1959: Sonny Liston, future heavyweight champion, won by a RTD 7 over Willi Besmanoff. Besmanoff had suffered several bad cuts over his eyes and had taken a pounding in the sixth round. The fight was ruled a seventh-round knockout. On the undercard of Ed Bang's annual Cleveland News Toyshop Fund Boxing Show, Solomon Boysaw won a 10-round unanimous decision over Candy McFarland, Cecil Shorts knocked out Antonio Marcilla in the sixth round, former Olympic champion Pete Rademacher won an eight-round decision over Johnny York, Tony Hughes won a six-round unanimous decision over John Hobart, Tony Christy won a four-round decision over Richie Craft, and Gene Jackson won a four-round split decision over Henry Hall, who was making his debut. The attendance was 7,710 with a gate of $27,897.50.

Calvin Butler was a local Golden Gloves champion who won the National Golden Gloves title in 1953 as a light-heavyweight. As a professional, he fought several times at the arena in the 1950s before retiring in 1964.

Tommy Salem was a local lightweight who squared up against some of the best fighters in the division, including Carlos Ortiz. From 1950 to 1955, he would fight at the arena six times.

Jake LaMotta floors Chuck Hunter and stops him with a sixth-round technical knockout victory on March 28, 1950. LaMotta, who was the middleweight champion at the time, had fought three previous fights at the arena in the 1940s and lost them all.

Future world lightweight champion Lauro Salas batters former world featherweight champion Sandy Saddler on the ropes during their April 18, 1950, fight for the world junior lightweight title, held by Saddler. Saddler stopped Salas at 2:51 of the ninth round to retain the championship.

Harry "Kid" Matthews was based out of Seattle and at various times had been a middleweight, light-heavyweight, and even heavyweight contender. In Cleveland, he fought Danny Nardico, who originally was from Painesville, Ohio, at the December 5, 1951, Cleveland News Toyshop Fund Boxing Show and won a 10-round unanimous decision. It was the only arena show of 1951.

Tony Anthony, who went on to become a light-heavyweight contender, made his professional ring debut on November 5, 1952, winning over George Boddie by RFD in the second round. Boddie was also making his ring debut.

Joe Brown, future World Lightweight Champion, knocked out Don Bowman in the first round on the December 10, 1952, Cleveland News Toyshop Fund Boxing Show. It was his only Cleveland appearance.

Kid Gavilan of Cuba was the world welterweight champion from 1951 to 1954. He fought twice at the arena, in 1950 and again in 1953, winning those fights against Livio Minelli and Tony Janiro of Youngstown, Ohio.

Johnny Bratton, former world welterweight champion, won a 10-round decision over Livio Minelli on May 7, 1953, in his only Cleveland appearance.

Gil Turner was a Philadelphia welterweight contender who lost in a title bid against champion Kid Gavilan in 1952 via an 11th-round technical knockout. In his one Cleveland Arena appearance, he lost a 10-round unanimous decision to Rocky Castellani on December 9, 1953, on a Cleveland News Toyshop Fund Boxing Show card.

Heavyweight Charlie Norkus of New Jersey fought an exciting 10-round battle with Roland LaStarza at the December 1, 1954, Cleveland News Toyshop Fund Boxing Show. LaStarza was the favorite, but Norkus pulled out a unanimous decision.

Tommy "Hurricane" Jackson, heavyweight contender, defeated former heavyweight champion Ezzard Charles on August 31, 1955, by a 10-round unanimous decision. Jackson later lost in a bid for Floyd Patterson's heavyweight crown by a technical knockout in the 10th round on July 29, 1957.

Mike DeJohn, a Buffalo, New York, heavyweight, met Jimmy Bivins on October 28, 1955, and lost a six-round decision. This was Jimmy Bivins's 112th and final professional bout in his career.

Bob Baker, a Pittsburgh heavyweight contender, had two quality wins at the arena in the 1950s, defeating Abel Cestac of Argentina on December 4, 1950, by a 10-round unanimous decision and Cuban Nino Valdez on December 7, 1955, also by a 10-round decision. Both were on Cleveland News Toyshop Fund Boxing Show cards.

Eduardo Lausse of Argentina was a middleweight contender who fought from 1947 to 1960. His one appearance at the Cleveland Arena was on December 7, 1955, when he defeated Johnny Sullivan by a TKO 5.

Gene Fullmer, who would go on to become two-time world middleweight champion, fought once at the arena and ended Rocky Castellani's Cleveland win streak by edging Castellani via a 10-round split decision on January 4, 1956.

Cleveland fighters who fought on the undercard of the main event between Joey Giardello and Charley Cotton on December 14, 1956, are pictured here. From left to right are Solomon Boysaw (lightweight), Cecil Shorts (welterweight), Joey Giardello (middleweight), Clarence Alford (middleweight), and Tony Hughes (heavyweight). All four Cleveland fighters won, as did Giardello. This was the annual Cleveland News Toyshop Fund Boxing Show.

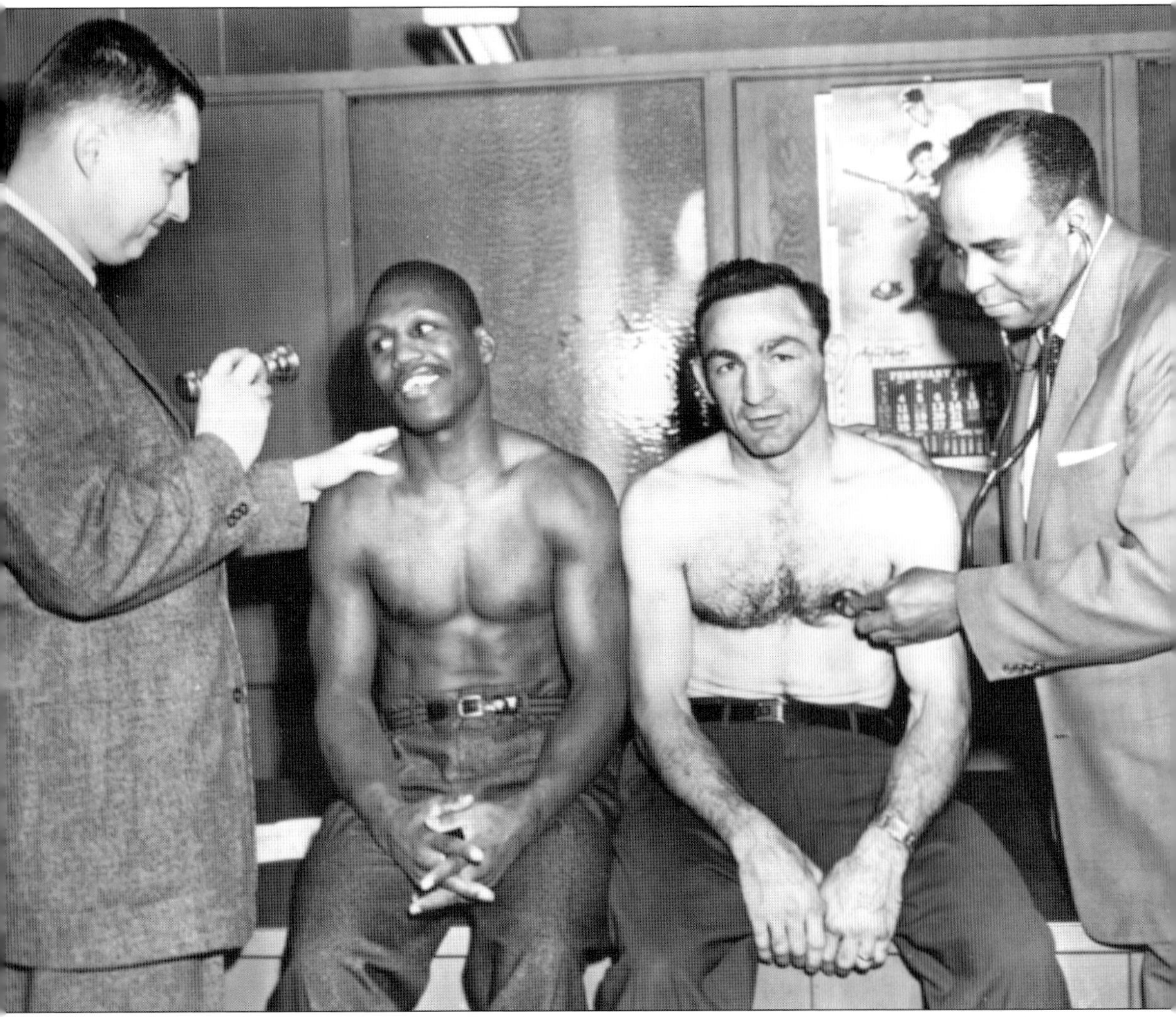

Carmen Basilio and Johnny Saxton get checked out by commission doctors prior to their February 22, 1957, title match at the arena.

Carmen Basilio, then world welterweight champion, defended his title by knocking out former champion Johnny Saxton in the second round. This was the first live fight the author ever attended.

Carmen Basilio was a two-time world welterweight champion and world middleweight champion. He was known as the "Upstate Onion Farmer" from upstate New York. His February 22, 1957, welterweight title match against former champion Johnny Saxton was his only appearance in Cleveland.

On February 22, 1957, Johnny Saxton, former welterweight champion, is weighed in by Cleveland boxing commissioner David Ott as champion Carmen Basilio watches. This was their rubber match, and Basilio won by a second-round knockout to retain his title.

Johnny Saxton was a two-time world welterweight champion. He only fought one time at the arena but was one of 50 champions who fought on arena fight cards from 1937 to 1973.

Dick Wagner was a Portland, Oregon, light-heavyweight contender who appeared on six arena cards. He had some very exciting matches with Artie Levine, Chuck Hunter, and Billy Fox in the 1940s and 1950s.

Solomon Boysaw was an outstanding lightweight who often traveled overseas to get fights. He did appear at the Cleveland Arena 10 times from 1956 to 1959, winning each of those fights.

Isaac Logart was a very tough Cuban welterweight contender who met the best in the division. Logart appeared at the Cleveland News Toyshop Fund Boxing Show on December 6, 1957, and won a 12-round unanimous decision over Gaspar Ortega. The bout was listed as a world welterweight eliminator.

Larry Boardman of Connecticut was a highly ranked lightweight who lost to Cleveland's Cecil Shorts by a 10-round unanimous decision at the annual Cleveland News Toyshop Fund Boxing Show on December 6, 1957. It was his only local appearance.

LuLu Perez fought at the arena during the December 6, 1957, Cleveland News Toyshop Fund Boxing Show, losing to Cleveland lightweight sensation Solomon Boysaw by an eight-round decision.

Mickey Mars was a local Golden Gloves champion who as a featherweight fought eight times at the arena in the 1950s.

Gabriel "Flash" Elorde, future junior lightweight champion, fought Cleveland's Solomon Boysaw on July 29, 1959, and lost a 10-round decision to the Cleveland hopeful. Three years later, they would meet again in Manila, Philippines, and Elorde would win a 10-round nontitle bout against Boysaw.

Shown here is a December 9, 1959, *Plain Dealer* promotion for the heavyweight match-up between future champion Sonny Liston and Willi Besmanoff at the Cleveland News Toyshop Fund Boxing Show. The referee stopped the fight after the sixth round as Besmanoff had suffered several bad cuts and had taken a beating. It went as a seventh-round technical knockout. (Caricature by Fred Reinhert, *Plain Dealer*.)

Five

The 1960s

If the 1950s seemed like lean years for Cleveland boxing then the 1960s must have seemed like the end of the line. The 37 shows in the previous decade seemed very successful compared to only 11 shows in the 1960s.

Larry Atkins was still doing most of the promoting and matchmaking, but a man named Oscar Kortowich did step in for two shows in November and December 1962, drawing small crowds. Using mostly local talent and a few out-of-town fighters, it was said he lost money on both promotions.

On December 13, 1960, Larry Atkins held what turned out to be the 35th and last Cleveland News Toyshop Fund Boxing Show. In 1960, the *Cleveland News* went out of business, basically being sold to the rival *Cleveland Press*, but never publishing again as the *Cleveland News*. At this last Christmas show, Larry Atkins had Pete Rademacher meeting Willi Besmanoff in the main event and local fighters Clarence Alford and Gene Jackson helping fill the undercard. This was also the end of Ed Bang's involvement in boxing and the end of his 53 years as sports editor for the *Cleveland News*. Ed Bang had worked at smaller papers before being hired in 1907 and succeeded Grantland Rice as sports editor.

The 1960s did have a few very good fight shows, including several this author was able to attend: the two Joey Giardello-Rocky Rivero nontitle fights in April and May 1964 and the final Gillette Friday Night Fight show on September 11, 1964, featuring Dick Tiger and Don Fullmer.

There were no fight shows at the Cleveland Arena from September 1964 until October 29, 1969, when Don Elbaum started holding fights there beginning with the Doyle Baird-Don Fullmer main event on October 29. That was the first Don Elbaum show this author attended at the Cleveland Arena.

Don Elbaum held two more shows in November and December 1969 in what could be called the beginning of the last great era in professional boxing in Cleveland.

All fight shows of the 1960s are listed here as they were seen by boxing fans at Cleveland Arena.

March 16, 1960: Ike Chestnut won a 10-round unanimous decision over Leroy Jeffery. Chestnut was down in the seventh round. The referee was Tony LaBranch. In other bouts, Cleveland heavyweight Tony Hughes won a six-round unanimous decision over Jackie Richards, and Floyd Joyner stopped Gene Jackson by a TKO 3, when referee Joe Sedley stopped the contest. Ronnie Cohen won by a KO over Robert Scott, Ernest Burford won by a TKO 4 over Lou Staton, and Frank Trusso won by a technical decision (TD 3) over Johnny Howard.

December 13, 1960: Pete Rademacher won by a 10-round unanimous decision over Willi Besmanoff. Scores were 47-43, 48-42, and 49-42. On the undercard, Cleveland welterweight Cecil Shorts stopped Vince Martinez by a TKO 4. The time was 2:46 when referee Jackie Davis stopped the contest. In other bouts, Cleveland middleweight Clarence Alford stopped Arley Seifer by a TKO in the third round; Johnny Bizzarro won a six-round decision over Jerry Wells; Jim Olive, in his debut, won a four-round unanimous decision over Joe Shelton; Teddy Grice won by a KO 4 over Billy Lowery; and Cleveland's heavyweight Gene Jackson won by a TKO 3 over Ted Davis. Matchmakers were Ed Bang and Larry Atkins. This was the 35th annual Cleveland News Toyshop Fund Boxing Show and the final one.

November 2, 1962: Alex Ford, local light-heavyweight, stopped Jim Christopher in the eighth round. In other bouts, Bert Whitehurst knocked out Joe Shelton in the fourth round, Dick Wipperman won by a KO 5 over Billy Lewis, Cleveland middleweight Earl Johnson won a six-round decision over Jodie James, Marion Conner won by a TKO 3 over Tom Bell, and Ramon DeLeon (ring debut) won a four-round split decision over Gary Conklin. The new promoter was Oscar Kortowich, and attendance was announced as 2,731.

December 21, 1962: Johnny Bizzarro won a 10-round unanimous decision over Neto Villareal. Scoring was 49-41, 48-41, and 49-44. In other bouts, Willie Williams won by a TKO 6 over Grant "Moose" Downing, and Marion Conner won by a KO 1 over Young Sam Langford. The time was 0:59. Chuck Tolliver won a four-round decision over Carl Polk; Roland Wilkes won a four-round unanimous decision over Larry Adams, who was making his debut; and Ramon DeLeon won by a KO 3 over Jerome Ware, who was also making his debut. The promoter was Oscar Kortowich.

January 17, 1964: Zora Folley won a 10-round unanimous decision over Canadian George Chuvalo. The scoring was as follows: referee Tony LaBranch, 50-45; judge Charley Bill, 49-42; and judge Bill Thompson, 47-44. In other bouts, Cincinnati heavyweight Billy Joiner won a 10-round decision over Lou Bailey, Fernand Chretien won a six-round decision over Brian O'Shea, Doug Agin won a four-round decision over James Twyman, Norman Smith won by a KO 3 over Dave Merritt, and Rory O' Shea won by a KO 1 over Charley Fell. The fights were promoted by Larry Atkins, and attendance was 5,415.

April 17, 1964: World middleweight champion Joey Giardello won a 10-round split decision over Juan "Rocky" Rivero. The scoring was as follows: referee Tony LaBranch, 46-45; judge Charley Bill, 45-46; and judge Bill Thompson, 46-45. Former middleweight champion Rocky Graziano was in Giardello's corner, and former heavyweight champion Rocky Marciano was in Rivero's corner. On the undercard, Johnny Bizzarro won by a KO 2 over Ricky Palmieri, Billy Joiner won an eight-round unanimous decision over Cody Jones, Earl Johnson won by a TKO 4 over Don "Honey Boy" Whitney, Fernand Chretien won a six-round split decision over Wesley Kidd, and Doug Agin won by a KO 2 over Lewis Parnell. The promoter was Larry Atkins, and attendance was 4,128 with a gate of $16,816.

May 22, 1964: Joey Giardello won a rematch over Rocky Rivero by a 10-round unanimous decision. Scoring was referee Mike Minnich, 46-43; judge Bill Thompson, 46-45; and judge Herb

Williams, 45-44. In other bouts, Billy Joiner won by a TKO 8 over Oron Johnson; Amos Johnson by a 10-round unanimous decision over Cody Jones; Doug Akin won a six-round unanimous decision over Sean Curtin; and Bobby Sandello, in his ring debut, won by a KO 1 over Ted Hackett. The time was 1:20 of the round. Former champs Joe Louis and Jersey Joe Walcott worked as referees on the undercard. Ezzard Charles, former heavyweight champion, was also in attendance and said, "Best fight card I have seen in years." The promoter was Larry Atkins, and attendance was 3,730.

September 11, 1964: In the final Friday Night Fight, Dick Tiger, former middleweight champion, defeated Don Fullmer by a 10-round unanimous decision. Scoring for the bout was as follows: referee Tony LaBranch, 49-43; judge Charley Bill, 48-42; and judge Herb Williams, 50-43. Fullmer's nose bled for a good portion of the fight. He had his brother Gene Fullmer, who lost his middleweight title to Dick Tiger, working his corner. The undercard featured heavyweight Amos Johnson of Medina, Ohio, winning a 10-round split decision over Billy Joiner; Cecil Shorts, a Cleveland welterweight, defeated Doug McLeod by a six-round decision; Earl Johnson once again defeated Don "Honey Boy" Whitney, this time by a four-round decision; Willie McMillian won a four-round decision over Jim Berdis; and Bobby Sandello won by a KO 3 over Carlos Bowers, who was making his debut. Don Dunphy was at the mike for this final Friday Night Fight broadcast as a small crowd of 1,796 watched the action. The promoter was Larry Atkins.

October 29, 1969: Doyle Baird of Akron won a hard fought 10-round split decision over third-ranked Don Fullmer. Scoring was referee Don Gonzales, 46-44; judge John Fayonek, 47-43; and judge Tony LaBranch, 46-47. Baird was handicapped by a deep cut over his left eye the last two rounds, which required 13 stitches to close. In other bouts, Cleveland lightweight Chuck Spencer stopped Willie Williams, also of Cleveland, via a third round knockout; "Irish" Billy Wagner, a Cleveland light-heavy, won by a TKO 4 over Jimmy Cherrico; Ted Gullick knocked out Lee Estes in the opening round; Hank Pelow won by a KO 1 over Joey Blair; and Julie Mandell won by a KO 4 over Andy Helmeczy. This was the beginning of the Don Elbaum era at the Cleveland Arena. Attendance was 4,873 with a gate of $23,000. Baird took home $5,142, while Fullmer got $6,000.

November 19, 1969: Alvin "Blue" Lewis won a 10-round unanimous decision over Bill McMurray. In other bouts, Gill King won by a TKO 7 over Tommy Kristian; Bill Hardney lost an eight-round split decision to Collinwood's "Irish" Billy Wagner; Earl Johnson stopped Kenny Partlow by a TKO in round two (time 1:40); Ted Gullick won by a KO 2 over Fred Askew (time 2:15); and Bobby Haymon, a Cleveland welterweight, won a six-round unanimous decision over Gene Masters.

December 10, 1969: Ray Anderson lost by a KO 9 to heavyweight hopeful Ted Gullick at 2:52 of that round. Other bouts featured Willie McMillian winning by a TKO in the first round over Vic Brown (time 2:40), Earl Johnson taking the bout by an eight-round unanimous decision over Garry Broughton, and Gil King winning by a TKO 4 over Tony Aquilar (time 1:37). Jimmy Tielsch won his debut by a KO 2 over Bobby Jackson, also making his debut.

In his very first professional fight, Pete Rademacher, Olympic gold medal winner at heavyweight in 1956, met champion Floyd Patterson (in a non–Cleveland Arena bout) for the heavyweight championship, losing by a sixth-round kayo on April 22, 1957. He fought twice at the arena, first in 1959 and again in 1960, winning both times by decision.

Clarence Alford was a Cleveland middleweight who fought at the arena six times during his career, which spanned the 1950s and 1960s. He had a good local following as most Cleveland fighters did. (Photograph by Perry Craig.)

George Chuvalo, a Canadian boxer, fought every top heavyweight in his career from 1956 to 1978, including Joe Frazier, George Foreman, and Muhammad Ali twice. His only Cleveland Arena appearance was on January 17, 1964, when he lost a 10-round unanimous decision to Zora Folley.

Zora Folley was a longtime heavyweight contender whose only appearance at the arena was on January 17, 1964, winning a 10-round unanimous decision over Canada's George Chuvalo.

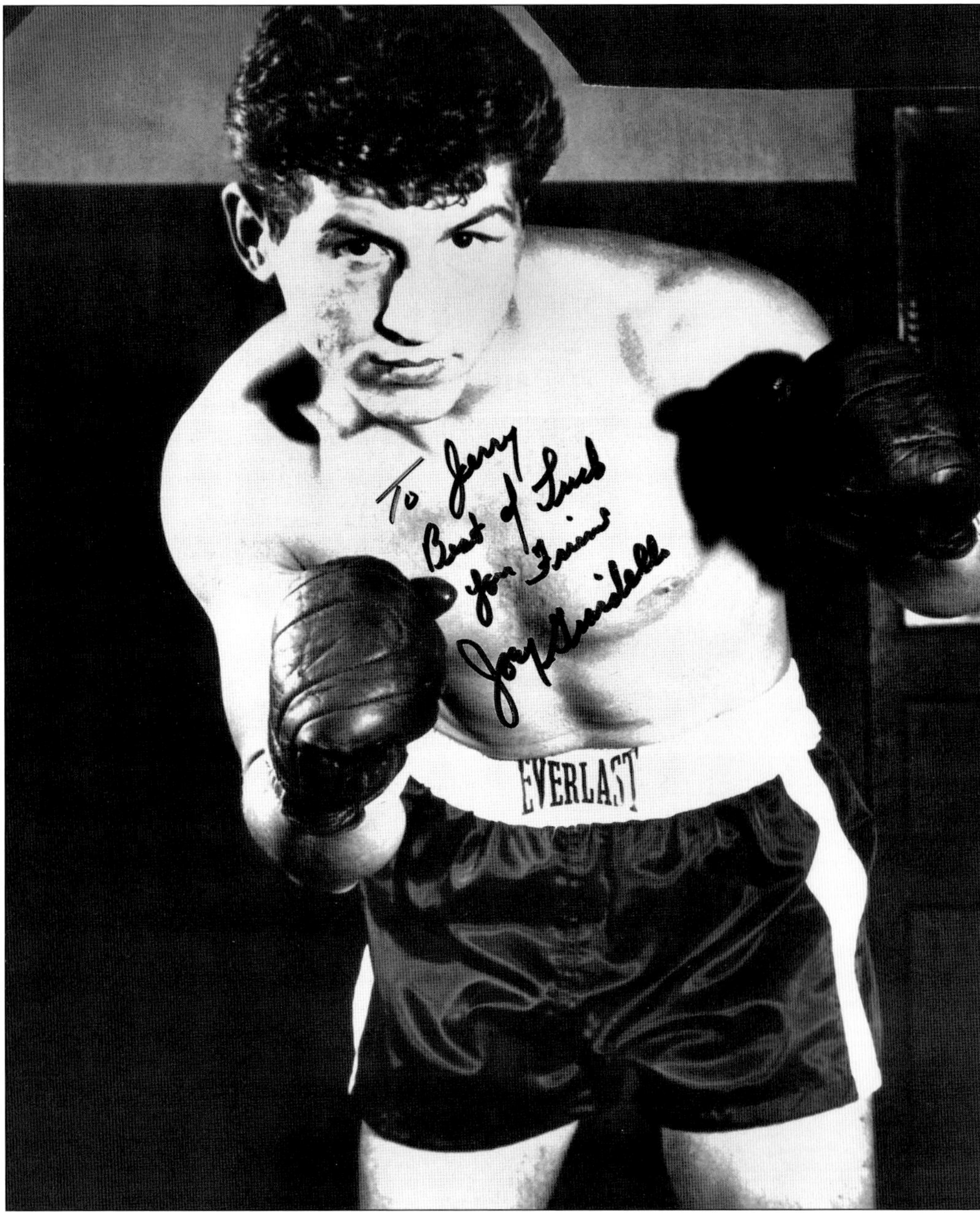

Joey Giardello, world middleweight champion, was a Cleveland favorite who fought seven times at the arena from 1956 to 1964 and won them all. He said Cleveland was his lucky town.

World middleweight champion Joey Giardello signs his contract to fight Rocky Rivero on April 17, 1964. With Giardello is Larry Atkins (left), famed promoter/matchmaker, and Cleveland boxing commissioner David Ott.

Jimmy Bivins, Joe Louis, and Ezzard Charles—three former heavyweight rivals—pose ringside at the Cleveland Arena for the May 22, 1964, Joey Giardello-Rocky Rivero rematch fight.

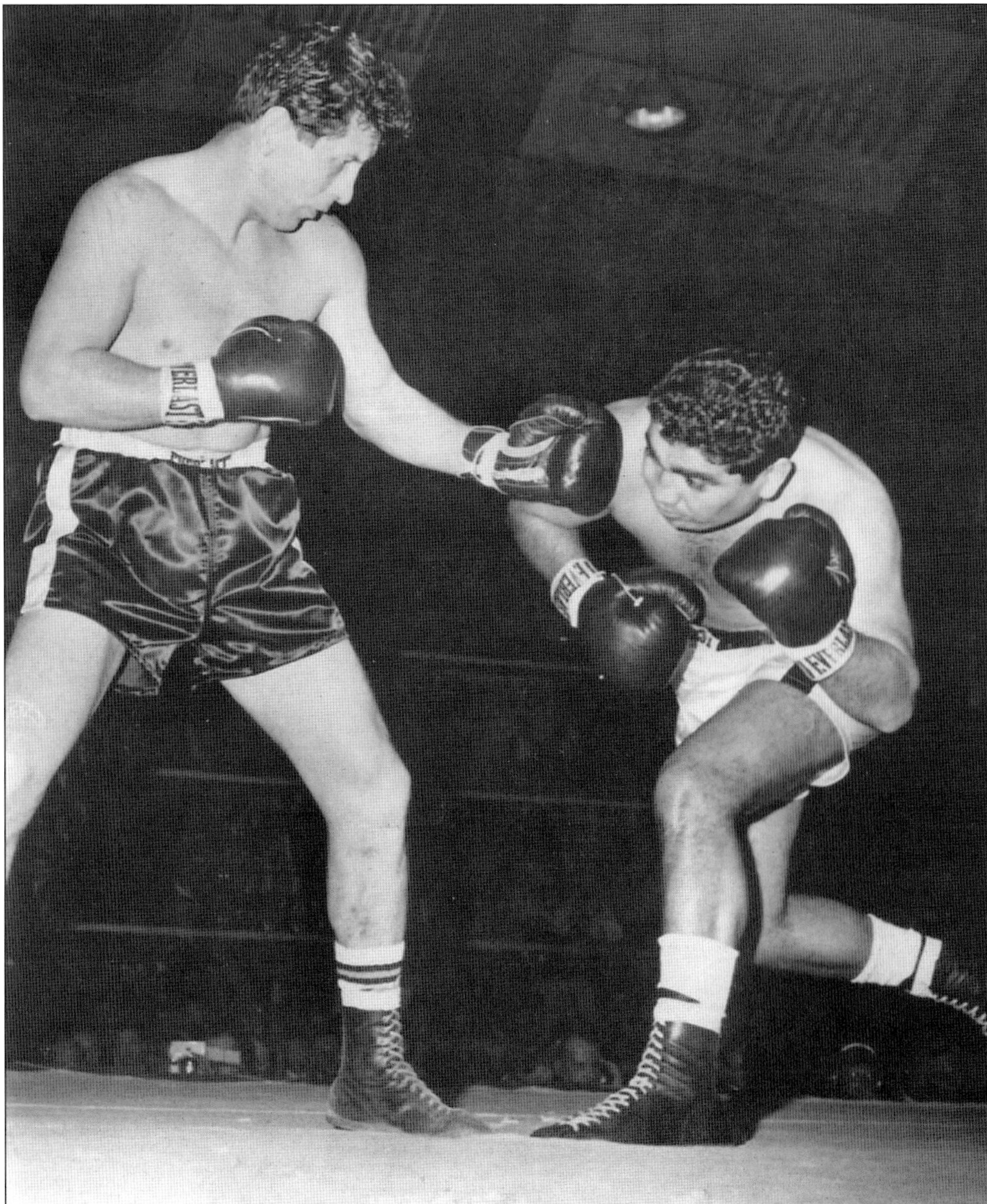

Joey Giardello (left) and Rocky Rivero (right) exchange punches during their second nontitle fight on May 22, 1964, a 10-round unanimous decision win for Giardello. In this fight, former middleweight champion Rocky Graziano was in Giardello's corner, and former heavyweight champion Rocky Marciano was in Rivero's corner.

Cecil Shorts rose from the Golden Gloves as the 1956 open division champion at 135 pounds to become a very good welterweight as a professional from 1956 to 1964. Shorts had wins over Larry Boardman, Benny Kid Paret, Eddie Perkins, and Isaac Logart, and he knocked out Vince Martinez. Shorts fought at the Cleveland Arena nine times, including the very last Gillette Friday Night Fight televised on September 11, 1964.

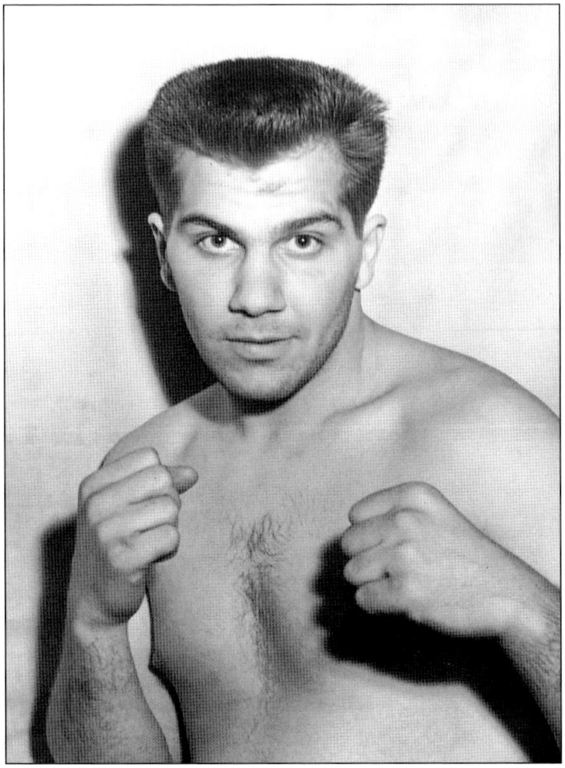

Tony Hughes was a local heavyweight backed by Teamsters Local 507. He had 30 professional bouts and fought at arena shows eight times from 1956 to 1963.

Doyle Baird, an Akron middleweight contender, fought seven times at the arena from 1969 to 1971, including matches with Emile Griffith and Mike Pusateri. His only title fight was at the arena on December 15, 1971, when he lost in his bid for the World Boxing Association (WBA) light-heavyweight title by an eighth-round technical knockout against champion Vicente Rondon.

Six

The 1970s

The 1960s were certainly not a great decade for boxing promotions at the Cleveland Arena. At the very end of the decade, Don Elbaum of Erie, Pennsylvania, came on the scene and sparked interest in boxing at the "old ice house," as some called the arena.

Don Elbaum gets credit for two things. The first was that he gave a lot of local fighters an opportunity to stay active and fight before their family and hometown friends. The names Billy Wagner, Doyle Baird, Tap Harris, Earl Johnson, Bobby Haymon, Frankie Kolovart, John Griffin, Terry Daniels, Chuck Spencer, Mike Harris, James Parks, and Ted Gullick are just some of the locals who fought numerous times for Don Elbaum. Baird and Griffin fought seven times each, and Billy Wagner, known as "Irish" Billy Wagner answered the call 14 times.

The second thing fight fans will always thank Don Elbaum for is bringing in famous fighters to the Cleveland Arena. Former champs Emile Griffith and Ernie Terrell performed here, future heavyweight champs Ken Norton and George Foreman fought here early in their careers, and in the last card ever held at the arena in 1973, a young Larry Holmes fought on the undercard. Contenders and former contenders such as Cleveland Williams, Roger Rouse, Don Fullmer, Mike Pusateri, and Hal "TNT" Carroll fought for Don Elbaum as well.

The very last fight card at the Cleveland Arena was on November 28, 1973. It was officially a Don King Production, his first as a promoter. But Don Elbaum was the guy who got him started and was matchmaker for this event that featured King's heavyweight hopeful, Jeff "Candy Slim" Merritt, who stopped Ron Stander in the third round by a TKO. Future heavyweight king Larry Holmes was on the undercard, stopping Kevin Isaac in the third round after being on the deck himself.

Shortly after the Don King/Don Elbaum fight show, the arena was shut down permanently in early 1974. It sat vacant for a few years and was finally knocked down in 1977 to make way for the local headquarters of the American Red Cross.

What memories!

Listed here in order are all the final fight cards and the last boxing action to appear before Cleveland fight fans at the arena in the 1970s.

January 28, 1970: Former three-time welterweight and two-time middleweight champion Emile Griffith won a 10-round unanimous decision over Akron's Doyle Baird. The scoring was as follows: referee Vito Mazzeo, 49-43; judge John Christopher, 47-43; and judge Tony LaBranch, 46-45. The supporting bouts featured Earl Johnson winning by a TKO 3 over Howard Youngblood (time 1:43); Billy Wagner knocking out Chico Corsey in the opening round; Bobby Haymon stopping Al Bashir at 1:57 of the opening round; and James Parks winning a six-round decision over Brian Green. Attendance was 7,104 with a gate of $45,131, of which Griffith received $15,000.

March 11, 1970: Chuck Spencer, a Cleveland bantamweight, won by a KO 6 over Eddie Santos in a bout for the North American bantamweight title. Heavyweight hopeful Ted Gullick stopped Tommy Hicks by a TKO 4. The time was 1:43 when referee John Christopher stopped the contest. In other bouts, Earl Johnson stopped Jimmy Ramos in the third round (time 1:45), Bobby Haymon won an eight-round unanimous decision over Adrian Davis, and Andy Helmeczy stopped Ernie Wicher in the opening round (time 0:38).

April 7, 1970: Future heavyweight champion Ken Norton stopped Bob Mashburn at 1:40 in the fourth round. On the undercard, Chuck Spencer won by a TKO 5 over Billy Brown; Vidal Flores won a 10-round decision over Vinnie Martinez; "Wild" Bill Hardney won an eight-round split decision over Billy Wagner; James Parks won an eight-round unanimous decision over Dave Thach; and Connie James won a four-round split decision over Harold Carter, who was making his professional debut.

April 29, 1970: Olympic champion and future heavyweight champion George Foreman won by a TKO 4 over Aaron Eastling. The time was 2:24. In other bouts, Ted Gullick stopped Lee Carr in the third round (time 2:58). Other bouts saw Billy Douglas winning a unanimous eight-round decision over James Parks, Billy Wagner claiming victory by a TKO 7 over Billy Marsh, Hank Pelow winning a six-round unanimous decision over Connie James, and John Mason winning by a TKO 2 over Joe Hestich (time 2:10).

May 27, 1970: Doyle Baird won a 10-round split decision over Doug Huntley. Scoring was 47-45, 43-47, and 48-45. On the undercard, Chuck Spencer won by a TKO 4 over Blas Viera (time 1:56). Bobby Haymon won by a KO 4 over Doug McLeod, Harold Carter won a six-round unanimous decision over Paul Nielsen, and Art Harris of Akron won a four-round unanimous decision over Willie Williams. It was the ring debut for Harris.

June 24, 1970: Chuck Leslie upset Ted Gullick, winning a 10-round majority decision, with scoring as follows: referee Mike Minnich, 46-45; Tony LaBranch, 47-43; and John Sayanek, 46-46. On the undercard, Chuck Spencer lost a 10-round split decision to Richie Gonzales, Bobby Haymon won an eight-round decision over Juan Ramos, Harold Carter and Paul Nielsen fought to a six-round draw, James Parks won by a KO 6 over Gene Simelton, and Art Harris won his second consecutive fight over Willie Williams with a four-round decision.

August 19, 1970: Ted Gullick won by a KO 9 over Johnny Hudgins; Jose Liano, substituting for Chuck Spencer, lost a 10-round decision to Richie Gonzales; and Billy Wagner stopped John Mason in the second round by a TKO. The time was 2:57. Al Bolden won a six-round decision over Harold Carter, Frankie Kolovart won a four-round decision over Willie Williams in his ring debut, and Art Harris won a four-round decision over Vic Thorpe.

September 30, 1970: Vic Brown won a 10-round unanimous decision over Leweni Waqa. In other bouts, "Irish" Billy Wagner stopped Paul Kasper by a TKO 3 (time 0:21). Earl Johnson won a 10-round unanimous decision over Fate Davis of Akron; James Parks, a Cleveland middleweight, won an eight-round decision over Hank Pelow; and Frankie Kolovart won by a TKO 1 over Larry Rossi. The time was 1:29.

November 25, 1970: Terry Daniels of Willoughby won by a TKO 6 over Paul Nielsen. Billy Wagner won a 10-round unanimous decision over former title challenger Roger Rouse, Frankie Kolovart won a six-round decision over Bob O'Neil, and Art Harris won a four-round unanimous decision over Vince Neratka.

December 15, 1970: Doyle Baird won a stunning second-round knockout over Cleveland's Earl Johnson. In other bouts, Terry Daniels won by a KO 2 over Joe Byrd, James Parks won a six-round decision over Jim Davis, Frankie Kolovart won a six-round decision over Joey Blair, and Willie Williams upset Dick Topinko by a six-round decision.

February 16, 1971: Billy Wagner stopped Karl Zurheide by a TKO 6. In the cofeature, Mike Pusateri upset Doyle Baird by a 10-round unanimous decision, flooring Baird in the final round. In other bouts, John Griffin, a light-heavyweight from Cleveland, won a 10-round unanimous decision over Willie McMillan; Ted Gullick knocked out Sylvester Dullaire in the fourth round; and Chuck Spencer won by a TKO 5 over Dick Divola (time 2:25).

March 31, 1971: John Griffin won a 10-round unanimous decision over "Irish" Billy Wagner in a battle of hometown light-heavyweight rivals. Doyle Baird won a return match with Mike Pusateri, stopping him on cuts in the third round. In other bouts, Cleveland welterweight Bobby Haymon won an eight-round unanimous decision over Premus Williams, Frankie Kolovart won a six-round decision over Terry Summerhays, and Dick Topinko won a six-round decision over Clevelander Jeff Morgan.

April 28, 1971: Former WBA heavyweight champion Ernie Terrell won a 10-round unanimous decision over Vic Brown. In other bouts, former title contender Cleveland Williams knocked down Ted Gullick in the 10th round and won a majority decision. Scoring was as follows: referee Mike Minnich, 46-46; judge Jimmy Bivins, 48-46; and judge Tony LaBranch, 47-43. In other bouts, Frankie Kolovart won an eight-round unanimous decision over Dick Topinko, Art Harris of Akron won by a TKO 5 over Otis Goode, and Chuck Wilburn stopped Mike Harris by a KO at 1:41 in the second round.

May 26, 1971: Former two-time world heavyweight champion Floyd Patterson won a 10-round unanimous decision over local heavyweight hopeful Terry Daniels, who was knocked down twice. Scoring was 49-41, 50-41, and 50-40. In other bouts, Frankie Kolovart knocked out Chuck Hernandez in the second round, Art Harris of Akron won an eight-round decision over Dick Topinko, Ralph Correa stopped Bobby Haymon by a TKO in the sixth, Lavern Lee Martin won a four-round decision over Harold Carter, and Ray Carrington won a four-round decision over Willie Williams. Attendance was 5,789 with a gate of $40,924. Patterson was paid $15,000.

June 29, 1971: Giant Jack O'Halloran lost a unanimous decision to substitute John Griffin of Cleveland. O'Halloran weighed 245 pounds to Griffin's 183, but it was no contest. Ralph Correa stopped Mike Pusateri by a TKO 5, Frankie Kolovart won an eight-round split decision over Nick Peoples, and Steve Jones stopped J.D. Williams in the third round at 2:19. Williams was making his debut.

October 19, 1971: In the main event, Don Fullmer, brother of Gene, won a 10-round unanimous decision over "Irish" Billy Wagner. In the cofeature, Terry Daniels won by a TKO 3 over Ted Gullick. The time was 1:26. In other bouts, Art Harris won by an eight-round unanimous decision over Fred Jimenez, Mike Harris won a six-round decision over Ray Carrington, and George Elias won by a KO 1 over Tommy Russell.

December 15, 1971: Vicente Rondon, WBA world light-heavyweight champion, defended his title with an eighth-round TKO over Doyle Baird. The time of the round was 2:20 when referee John Christopher stopped the contest after Baird had been down three times. Scoring at the time was 33-31, 33-31, and 34-30 in favor of Rondon. On the undercard, John Griffin was upset by a TKO 7 against Vic Brown. The time was 2:37. Frankie Kolovart won a six-round unanimous decision over Sammy Maul, and Mike Harris won a six-round decision over Ray Carrington.

February 8, 1972: John Griffin stopped "Irish" Billy Wagner in the 12th and final round. The time was 2:01 when referee John Christopher stopped the fight. Wagner had built up a huge lead until hurt and floored by a Griffin left hook. Referee Christopher had Wagner winning 52-51, judge Tony LaBranch favored Wagner 53-48, and judge Jimmy Bivins had Wagner winning 55-51 at the time of the stoppage. Griffin took home $2,500, or 20 percent of the gate, while Wagner got a flat guarantee of $4,500. The *Plain Dealer* card showed Wagner winning 53-46 heading into the last round. In other bouts, Art Harris remained undefeated as he won an eight-round unanimous decision over Sammy Maul, Bobby Haymon won by a TKO 6 over Jesus Alicia, and Levern Le Martin won a sixth-round unanimous decision over Charlie Jordan. Attendance was 2,288, and the gate was $13,900.

April 26, 1972: John Griffin won a 10-round unanimous decision over Ray White. The referee was Jackie Keough. The undercard saw Cleveland's Frankie Kolovart losing a 10-round unanimous decision to Art "Tap" Harris of Akron, and Cleveland welterweight Bobby Haymon winning by a KO 2 over Jose Pagan Rivera.

August 28, 1972: John Griffin, a Cleveland light-heavyweight, defeated heavyweight Sam McGill by a six-round split decision. Billy Wagner won a six-round unanimous decision over Joe Cokes, and Art Harris won by a TKO 5 over Marcelino Alicia. Before the scheduled fights put on by Don Elbaum, Don King held an exhibition featuring Muhammad Ali to raise funds for Forest City Hospital (since closed). Ali boxed two rounds each against heavyweights Vic Brown, Alonzo Johnson, and Amos Johnson and four rounds against Terry Daniels. Along with pre-show entertainment Don King provided, the Ali show pushed Don Elbaum's fight card to a late start, and there was only time for six-round bouts. Attendance was 8,572, and the gate was $81,250.

November 29, 1972: "Irish" Billy Wagner won a 10-round split decision over Hal "TNT" Carroll. Scoring was referee John Christopher 47-46 for Wagner, judge Jimmy Bivins 50-46 for Carroll, and judge Ed McGuire 47-46 for Wagner. On the undercard, Bobby Haymon won by a disqualification (DQ) in the fourth round over Terry Hayward. The time was 2:37 when referee Don Gonzalez stopped the fight. Billy "Dynamite" Douglas won by a TKO 8 over Marion Conner, and Harold Carter and Dave Matthews fought to a 10-round draw. The promoter for this card was Bruce Trampler. Attendance was listed as 750, one of the smallest arena crowds ever.

November 28, 1973: In Don King's first professional fight card, light-heavyweights Ray Anderson of Akron and Jimmy Dupree of Jersey City fought to a 10-round draw. In the main event, Jeff "Candy Slim" Merritt manhandled Ron Stander, stopping him by a TKO in the third round when referee Lew Eskin halted the contest. The time was 0:41. Stander had been down three times in the second round. It was a totally one-sided fight. Merritt weighed 218 pounds, and Stander came in at a hefty 245 pounds. In other bouts, Chuck Spencer won an eight-round unanimous decision over Pedro Guzman; Larry Holmes, future heavyweight champion, got off the floor to stop Kevin Isaac by a TKO at 1:05 of the third round; and Rocky Bonilla won a six-round unanimous decision over Julie Mandell. Although this was a Don King Production, Don Elbaum was the matchmaker for the show. Attendance was listed as 4,857 for what turned out to be the last fight promotion ever held at the Cleveland Arena. By 1974, the arena shut down for good to all events, and in 1977, it was torn down. In its place today sits the local headquarters of the American Red Cross.

Don Elbaum of Erie, Pennsylvania, was a promoter/matchmaker who made his mark in the Cleveland/Akron area from 1968 to 1973. From 1969 to 1972 at the Cleveland Arena, he put on 24 shows. (Photograph by Kipp Elbaum.)

The Don Elbaum fight card from February 16, 1971, featured local fighters who appeared in the ring that night. When all was said and done, Don Elbaum—in the short period of time he was promoting in Cleveland—put on 24 shows at the Cleveland Arena, counting the three in 1969. The second-to-last show at the arena on November 29, 1972, was promoted by Bruce Trampler. Sadly, that fight card only drew 750 people.

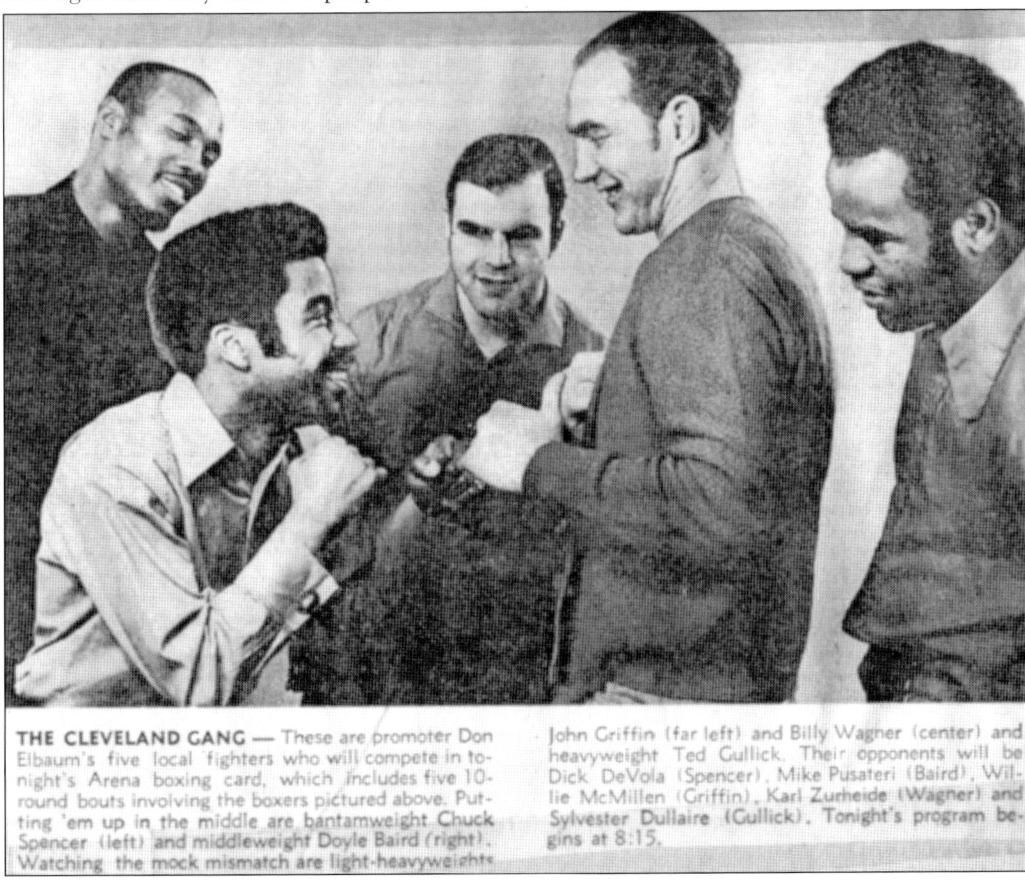

THE CLEVELAND GANG — These are promoter Don Elbaum's five local fighters who will compete in tonight's Arena boxing card, which includes five 10-round bouts involving the boxers pictured above. Putting 'em up in the middle are bantamweight Chuck Spencer (left) and middleweight Doyle Baird (right). Watching the mock mismatch are light-heavyweights John Griffin (far left) and Billy Wagner (center) and heavyweight Ted Gullick. Their opponents will be Dick DeVola (Spencer), Mike Pusateri (Baird), Willie McMillen (Griffin), Karl Zurheide (Wagner) and Sylvester Dullaire (Gullick). Tonight's program begins at 8:15.

Billy Wagner fought under the name "Irish" Billy Wagner as a light-heavyweight. From 1969 to 1972, he fought for promoter Don Elbaum more times than any other fighter, appearing in 14 total bouts. Wagner was very popular, and the fact he worked as a *Plain Dealer* driver certainly did not hurt his popularity. The *Plain Dealer* was Ohio's largest newspaper. (Photograph by Norbert J. Yassanye, *Plain Dealer*.)

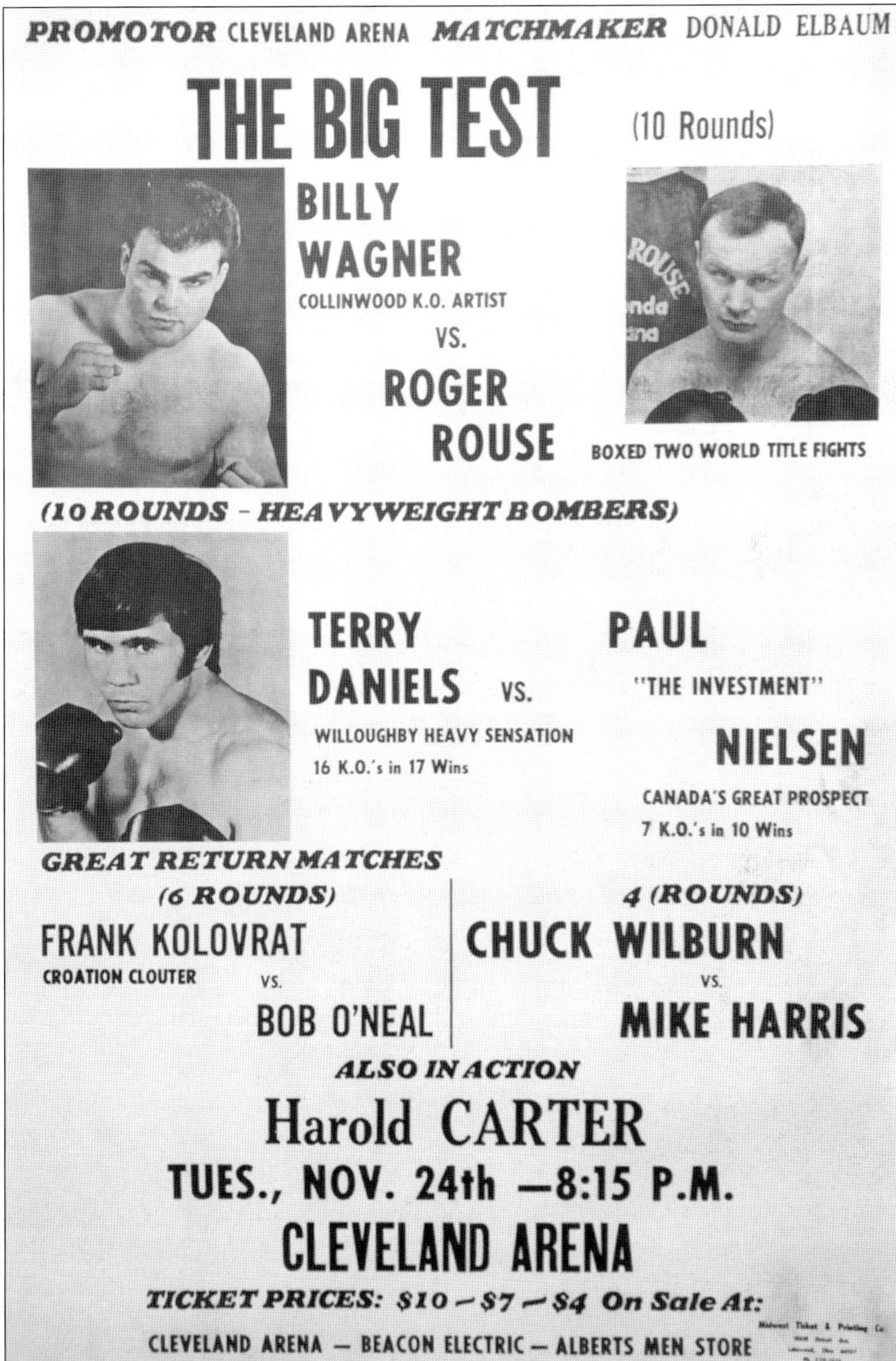

Pictured here is the arena fight card for November 24, 1970. (Courtesy of Will McCulloch.)

Doyle Baird and Emile Griffith pose prior to their January 28, 1970, ten-round fight at the arena. The show drew a crowd of 7,104. (Photograph by Dudley Brumbach, *Plain Dealer*.)

Emile Griffith was an excellent fighter who held the welterweight title three times and the middleweight title twice. His only appearance in Cleveland was on January 28, 1970, when he won a 10-round unanimous decision over Akron's Doyle Baird.

Vicente Rondon of Venezuela was WBA world light-heavyweight champion when he successfully defended his title against Akron's Doyle Baird on December 15, 1971, by an eighth-round technical knockout.

George Foreman, the 1968 Olympic gold medal winner in the heavyweight division and future two-time world heavyweight champion, appeared at the Cleveland Arena in his second year as a professional on April 29, 1970, knocking out Aaron Eastling in the fourth round.

Ken Norton would go on to hold a piece of the heavyweight title as WBC champion. He fought once at the Cleveland Arena in his early career on April 7, 1970, and knocked out Bob Mashburn in the fourth round at the 1:10 mark.

Joey Blair (left) and Frankie Kolovart (right) exchange punches during their December 15, 1970, bout, which was won by Kolovart in a six-round decision. Kolovart, born in Croatia, was a local welterweight favorite who fought in Don Elbaum's shows nine times. (Photograph by George Heinz, *Plain Dealer*.)

Mike Pusateri (left) and Doyle Baird (right) pose before their first bout on February 16, 1971. Pusateri won a 10-round unanimous decision over the Akronite. (Photograph by Charles Harris, *Plain Dealer*.)

Pictured here is the arena fight card for the show on March 31, 1971. (Courtesy of Will McCulloch.)

Former heavyweight contender Cleveland Williams floors local hopeful Ted Gullick in the 10th and final round. Williams, at this late stage of his career, still had enough left to win this split decision on April 28, 1971. (Photograph by Dick Gluszek.)

Ernie Terrell, former WBA heavyweight champion, met Buffalo's Vic Brown in a 10-rounder on April 28, 1971. Terrell won a unanimous decision in a very dull bout with a lot of holding.

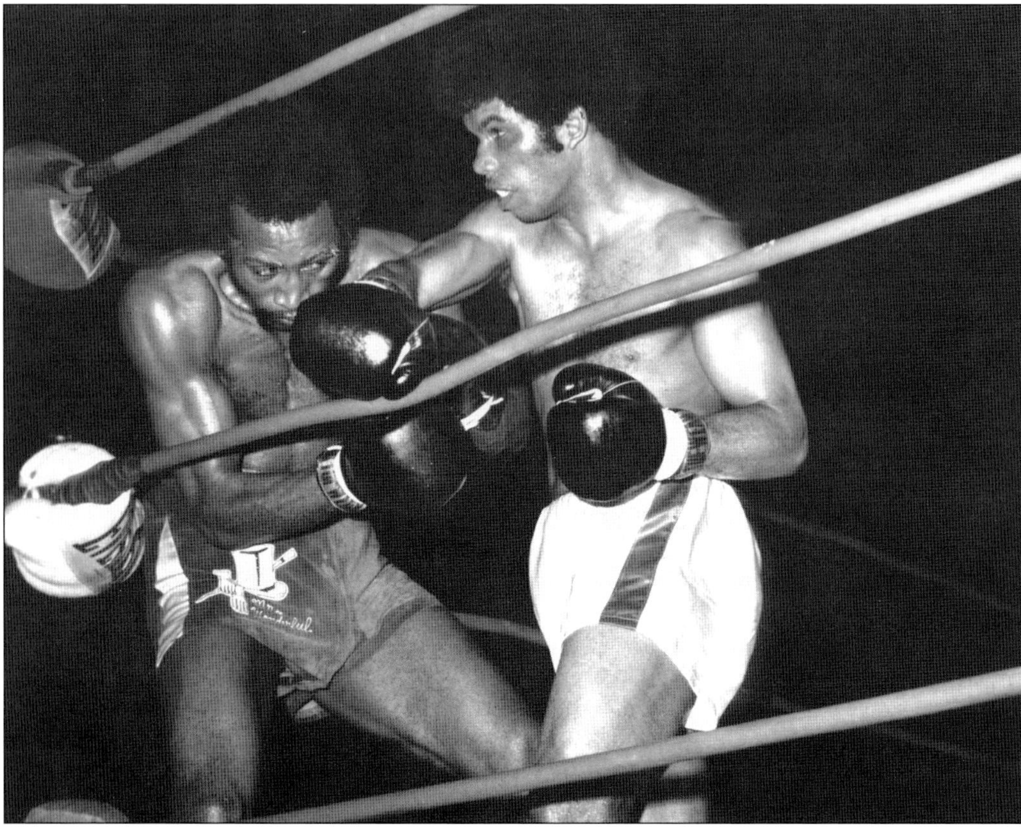

Ralph Correa lands a hard right hand on Cleveland welterweight Bobby Haymon in the sixth round on May 26, 1971. The fight was stopped moments later for a TKO win for Correa. (Photograph by Dick Gluszek.)

Floyd Patterson, the 1952 Olympic gold medal winner at middleweight and two-time world heavyweight champion, only appeared in Cleveland once, on his last comeback trail on May 26, 1971.

Floyd Patterson lands a leaping left hook on local heavyweight hopeful Terry Daniels. Patterson floored Daniels twice and won an easy 10-round decision on May 26, 1971. (Photograph by the author.)

Pictured here is the arena fight card for October 19, 1971. (Courtesy of Will McCulloch.)

James Parks was a local middleweight who had moderate success in the pros after coming out of the Golden Gloves. During his career from 1969 to 1978, he had 29 fights and fought on arena cards six different times in the 1970s.

"Irish" Billy Wagner was a very popular Collinwood fighter who came out of the local Golden Gloves with one title. He turned pro in 1968. As a light-heavyweight, he had 45 professional fights and fought on Don Elbaum's shows at the Cleveland Arena 14 times from 1969 to 1972.

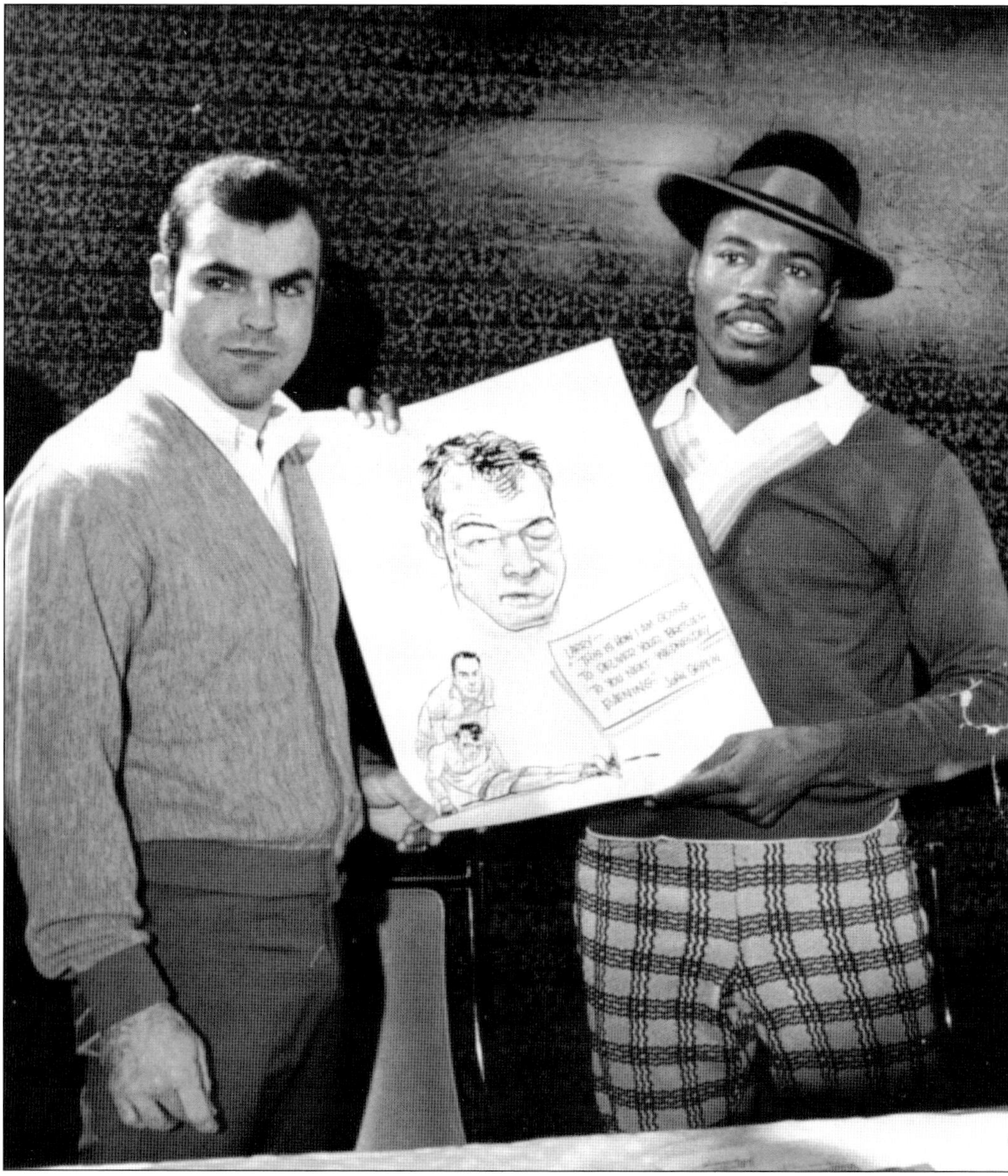

Billy Wagner and John Griffin, local light-heavyweights, pose for a prefight publicity shot for their February 8, 1972, rematch. (Photograph by Andrew Cifranic, *Plain Dealer*.)

Billy Wagner digs to the body of John Griffin during their 12-round grudge match on February 8, 1972. Wagner built up a huge lead only to be stopped in the final round at the 2:01 mark by a technical knockout. (Photograph by the author.)

Earl Johnson, known as "Sugarcane," was a local Golden Gloves champion who fought as a professional middleweight from 1962 to 1970. He fought nine times at the arena between 1969 and 1971, going 8-1 during the Don Elbaum era. His biggest win was against Akron's Fate Davis.

Larry Holmes was featured on the undercard of the Jeff Merritt-Ron Stander main event on November 28, 1973. Holmes got off the floor to stop Kevin Isaac at 1:05 of the third round for a TKO. Holmes would go onto greatness as world heavyweight champion. This was the last fight card held at the Cleveland Arena before it closed.

This Jeff Merritt and Ron Stander poster is advertising their November 28, 1973, fight at the Cleveland Arena. This would turn out to be the last fight card ever held at the arena before it closed for good in 1974.

Jeff Merritt and local referee Ronnie Tillman are pictured in the 1980s at an amateur show. Merritt had the distinction of fighting in the main event at the very last fight show ever held at the Cleveland Arena on November 28, 1973, when he knocked out Ron Stander in the third round. (Photograph by Terry Gallagher.)

The Cleveland Arena marquee, shown here in the1970s, captures the state of the old boxing mecca at the end of an irreplaceable era. Many major bouts and champion boxers were featured on this marquee. Although the arena did not open until November 1937, in its first three years one of the all-time great fighters, Henry Armstrong, appeared to defend his world welterweight title. The 1940s and 1950s had countless great fight cards, and even in the 1960s, there were some quality matches. The 1970s were short, ending in November 1973, but promoter Don Elbaum had some great fight cards featuring many local Cleveland fighters. He also brought in famous champions and contenders such as Emile Griffith, Floyd Patterson, Ken Norton, and George Foreman, just to name a few. From December 1937 until November 1973, a total of 162 fight cards were held at the Cleveland Arena—903 individual fights. Fifty champions fought on these cards. (Photograph by the author.)

This photograph of author Jerry Fitch was part of a feature story in the *Plain Dealer* sports section by writer Bob Dolgan in the newspaper's February 7, 1983, edition. Most fight fans were not fortunate to see many championship fights locally. Fitch was young but still fortunate to see Carmen Basilio take out Johnny Saxton in the second round in February 1957. In later years, he got to travel and see several championship fights in other cities and a few locally in the 1980s, during the Don King days in Cleveland. But his history of attending and eventually covering fights began at Cleveland Arena. He has authored or coauthored six previous titles: *Cleveland's Greatest Fighters of All Time* (2002), *James Louis Bivins: The Man Who Would Be Champion* (2011), *50 Years of Fights, Fighters and Friendships* (2013), *Johnny Risko: The Cleveland Rubber Man* (2016), *My Favorite Fights* (2018), and *A Few More Rounds: A Collection of Boxing Tales* (2020). (Photograph by Michael J. Zaremba, *Plain Dealer.*)

Champions at Cleveland Arena 1937–1973

This list includes champions who were partially recognized by various governing bodies, former champions, champions defending their titles, champions fighting a nontitle fight, and future champions.

Key
* = world recognition
** = WBA (World Boxing Association)
*** = Maryland
+ = NBA (National Boxing Association)
# = WBC (World Boxing Council)
NY = New York recognition

Muhammad Ali: fought 10-round exhibition *
Lou Ambers: two-time lightweight *
Joey Archibald: featherweight, NY
Henry Armstrong: featherweight, lightweight, welterweight *
Carmen Basilio: two-time welterweight and middleweight *
Melio Bettina: light-heavyweight * and NY
Johnny Bratton: welterweight +
Joe Brown: lightweight *
Ezzard Charles: heavyweight*
Anton Christoforidis: light-heavyweight +
Flash Elorde: junior lightweight *
George Foreman: two-time heavyweight *
Gene Fullmer: two-time middleweight *+
Ceferino Garcia: middleweight *
Kid Gavilan: welterweight *
Joey Giardello: middleweight *
Rocky Graziano: middleweight *
Emile Griffith: three-time welterweight and two-time middleweight *
Larry Holmes: heavyweight *#
Al Hostak: middleweight +
Izzy Jannazzo: welterweight ***
Harry Jeffra: bantam and featherweight *
Lew Jenkins: lightweight *
Solly Kreiger: middleweight +
Jake LaMotta: middleweight *
Gus Lesnevich: light-heavyweight *+
Sonny Liston: heavyweight *
Joe Louis: fought six-round exhibition with Jimmy Bivins *
Joey Maxim: light-heavyweight *
Archie Moore: light-heavyweight *
Ken Norton: heavyweight #
Ken Overlin: middleweight *
George Pace: bantamweight +
Floyd Patterson: two-time heavyweight *
Willie Pep: two-time featherweight *
Sugar Ray Robinson: welterweight and five-time middleweight *
Vicente Rondon: Light-heavyweight **
Sandy Saddler: two-time featherweight and junior lightweight *
Lauro Salas: lightweight *
Petey Sarron: featherweight *
Johnny Saxton: two-time welterweight *
Billy Soose: middleweight *
Phil Terranova: featherweight +
Ernie Terrell: heavyweight **
Dick Tiger: two-time middleweight and light-heavyweight *
Jersey Joe Walcott: heavyweight *
Ike Williams: lightweight *
Jackie Wilson: featherweight +
Chalky Wright: featherweight *
Teddy Yarosz: middle + and NY
Fritzie Zivic: welterweight *